AF655256

STEAM

Module for Students

The kid books

STEAM MODULE FOR STUDETNTS

ISBN : 978-81-19745-41-8

Publisher
Unbound Script
B-10, Seven Wonder Business Center
Plot No. G-20, Basement, Preet Vihar
New Delhi-110092
Website : www.unboundscript.com
Email : books@unboundscript.com

Compilation & Illustration - Unbound Script

Price: ₹ 599/-

Printed in India

PREFACE

Welcome to the captivating world of **STEAM** - **Science, Technology, Engineering, Arts, and Mathematics.** In this book, we embark on a journey through the intersections of these diverse disciplines, exploring their interconnectedness and their profound impact on our lives and the world around us. STEAM represents more than just individual subjects; it embodies a holistic approach to learning and problem-solving. It encourages **creativity, critical thinking,** and **innovation,** driving progress and shaping the future in remarkable ways. As we delve into the pages ahead, I invite you to open your mind to the possibilities that **STEAM** offers. Whether you're a student, educator, professional, or simply curious about the wonders of the world, there's something here for everyone. So, let's embark on this journey together, embracing the beauty of discovery and the thrill of exploration. Let's celebrate the diversity of **STEAM** and the endless opportunities it presents. Together, let's ignite our passion for learning and unleash our potential to make a difference. Enjoy the adventure.

CONTENTS

Science

Technology

Engineering

Arts

Maths

Science

Technology

Engineering

Arts

Maths

STEAM

SCIENCE

The Scientific Methods?

The scientific method is a systematic approach used by scientists to investigate natural phenomena, acquire new knowledge, and test hypotheses. It involves a series of steps that are followed below:

Observation: The process begins with observing and recognizing a phenomenon or problem in the natural world. This could be something noticed through direct observation, previous research, or everyday experiences.

Question: Based on the observation, a question is formulated. A question is a tentative explanation or prediction about the observed phenomenon. It should be testable and falsifiable.

Hypothesis: A hypothesis is proposed to explain the observed phenomenon. This is a statement that can be tested through experimentation or observation. It often takes the form of an "if-then" statement.

Experimentation: Controlled experiments are designed and conducted to test the hypothesis and gather data. In experiments, variables are manipulated and controlled to determine their effect on the outcome.

Conclusion: Conclusions are drawn regarding the validity of the hypothesis. The results are then interpreted in the context of the original question or problem.

Scientific Method

Directions: Color and cut out the puzzle pieces. Glue the puzzle pieces below according to where they belong with the scientific method.

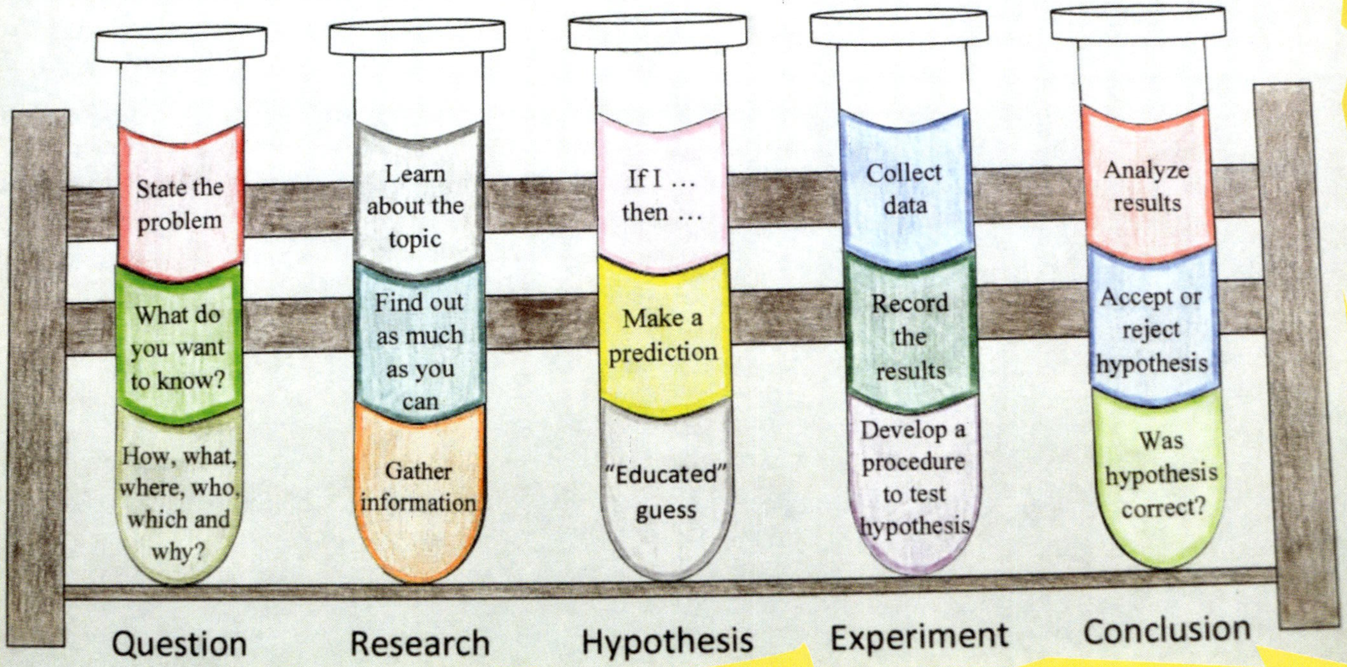

Scientists Rock!

Galileo was a scientist who lived a long time ago in Italy. He made a lot of important discoveries in astronomy, which is the study of stars and planets. He was the first person to use a telescope to look at the sky and discovered things like the moons of Jupiter and the rings of Saturn.

Galileo Galilei

Thomas Edison was an inventor and scientist who invented many things that changed the world, like the electric light bulb, the phonograph (which could record and play back sound), and the motion picture camera. He was always experimenting and trying to come up with new ideas to make life better.

Thomas Edison

Stephen Hawking was a theoretical physicist known for his work on black holes and the origins of the universe. Despite being diagnosed with a motor neuron disease at a young age, he made significant contributions to our understanding of the cosmos.

Stephen Hawking

Isaac Newton was a mathematician and physicist who discovered the laws of motion and gravity. He famously watched an apple fall from a tree, which inspired his ideas about gravity.

Isaac Newton

Ada Lovelace was a mathematician and writer known for her work on Charles Babbage's early mechanical general-purpose computer, the Analytical Engine. She is often regarded as the world's first computer programmer.

Ada Lovelace

Charles Darwin was a naturalist who developed the theory of evolution by natural selection. His book "On the Origin of Species" explained how species change over time through the process of natural selection.

Charles Darwin

The Smartest Person

Albert Einstein

was an amazing scientist who lived a long time ago. He was born in Germany in 1879 and became one of the most famous scientists in history.

Einstein was really, really smart! He came up with ideas that changed the way we understand the universe. His brain was so special that even after he died, scientists studied it to try to understand why he was so brilliant.

One of Einstein's biggest ideas was called the Theory of Relativity. It talks about how space and time are connected, and how things like gravity work. It sounds super complicated, but basically, it helped scientists understand how the universe works on a really big scale.

Einstein had really wild and curly hair! He also wore funny clothes, like baggy pants and mismatched socks. But even though he looked a little different, he was really respected for his brilliant mind.

Albert Einstein was not only a genius scientist but also a person who cared about making the world a better and more peaceful place.

He showed us that with curiosity, imagination, and hard work, we can understand the mysteries of the universe.

Famous Scientists Word Search

A	L	E	X	A	N	D	E	R	F	L	E	M	I	N	G	M
L	L	O	U	I	S	P	A	S	T	E	U	R	K	I	L	A
N	I	R	F	Q	Z	C	W	X	L	L	R	F	Z	B	A	R
I	S	G	Y	S	B	G	Y	H	G	K	Z	R	S	T	L	I
K	A	T	H	O	M	A	S	E	D	I	S	O	N	O	F	E
O	A	I	D	P	J	X	R	K	O	A	K	J	E	E	R	C
L	C	O	W	O	A	H	N	P	O	L	G	J	A	D	E	U
A	N	T	V	R	M	N	R	A	E	A	B	J	C	W	D	R
T	E	A	L	B	E	R	T	E	I	N	S	T	E	I	N	I
E	W	Y	H	M	S	E	X	O	O	T	S	H	B	N	O	E
S	T	B	E	E	W	Y	H	O	R	U	E	O	N	H	B	H
L	O	H	P	F	A	P	A	S	L	R	M	M	A	U	E	N
A	N	O	R	D	T	O	Z	S	D	I	Q	S	H	B	L	M
J	M	L	Q	E	S	U	S	B	X	N	A	O	I	B	L	S
N	S	B	H	Y	O	S	I	L	Q	G	S	N	R	L	P	X
M	D	M	H	E	N	O	B	E	I	M	M	V	N	E	P	J
E	R	N	E	S	T	R	U	T	H	E	R	F	O	R	D	G
M	B	U	A	U	V	T	C	L	B	W	F	E	H	V	W	P
Q	M	S	T	E	P	H	E	N	H	A	W	K	I	N	G	P
N	Y	V	O	F	N	F	C	W	T	W	L	R	N	F	T	R
X	H	V	S	X	R	Y	F	Y	A	S	K	X	R	T	H	C
C	H	A	R	L	E	S	D	A	R	W	I	N	J	U	Y	Q

ALBERT EINSTEIN	JJ THOMSON	ALEXANDER FLEMING
MARIE CURIE	CHARLES DARWIN	EDWIN HUBBLE
STEPHEN HAWKING	ALFRED NOBEL	ALAN TURING
LOUIS PASTEUR	THOMAS EDISON	JAMES WATSON
ISAAC NEWTON	NIKOLA TESLA	ERNEST RUTHERFORD

Our Plants

Hundreds of thousands of different species, or kinds, of plant grow on Earth. Some plants are so tiny that people can hardly see them. Others are trees that grow as tall as skyscrapers.

Most plants have several things in common. They need sunshine, water, and air to grow. They are not able to move around. Their cells have stiff walls made of a tough material called cellulose. All green plants use the Sun's energy, water,

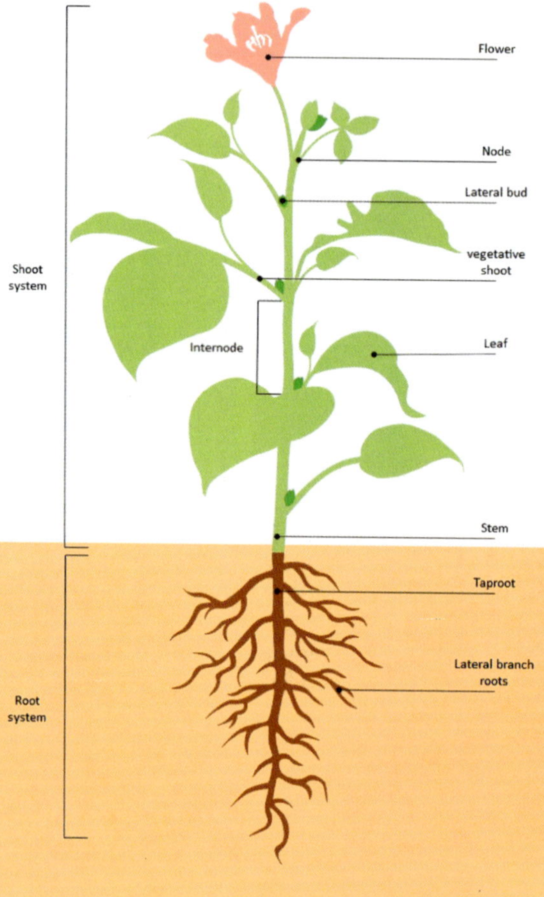

and a gas called carbon dioxide to make their own food. This process is called **photosynthesis.**

All plants belong to one of two main groups, vascular plants and nonvascular plants. Vascular plants have special tissues, called xylem and phloem, that carry water and food throughout the plant. Vascular plants also have roots, stems, and leaves. Vascular plants include herbaceous plants, shrubs, and trees. Herbaceous plants have soft stems. Shrubs and trees have woody stems.

Nonvascular plants do not have xylem or phloem. They also lack true roots, stems, and leaves. Nonvascular plants include mosses, liverworts, and hornworts. They are generally small and grow in moist places.

COLOUR IT

Photosynthesis

Photosynthesis is the process in which green plants use sunlight to make their own food. Photosynthesis is necessary for life on Earth. Without it there would be no green plants, and without green plants there would be no animals. Photosynthesis requires sunlight, chlorophyll, water, and carbon dioxide gas.

Chlorophyll is a substance in all green plants, especially in the leaves. Plants take in water from the soil and carbon dioxide from the air.

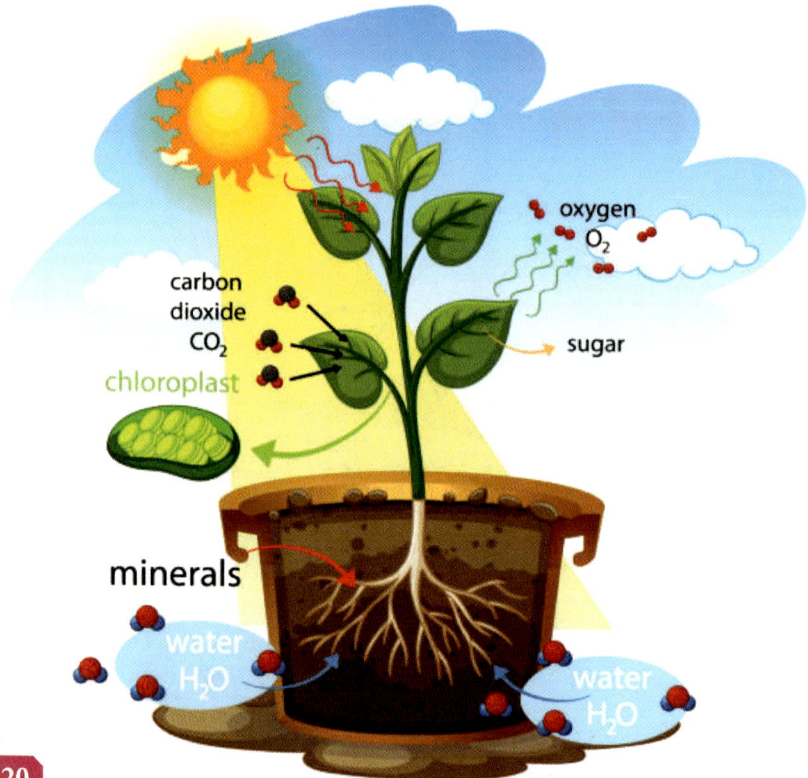

Baby Seeds

Seeds are like baby plants waiting to grow. Inside each seed is a tiny plant embryo, along with some food to help it get started. The outer covering of the seed protects the embryo and keeps it safe until it's ready to grow.

Colour the fruits which have few seeds.

Grouping Animals

There are a lot of animals in the world. Imagine you have a big bookshelf with lots of different books on it. You might organize the books into groups based on things like their size, color, or the type of story they tell. Scientists do something similar with animals! They group them based on similarities and differences.

Classify the animals by fur, feather, scales or skin :

(a) ____________

(b) ____________

(c) ____________

(d) ____________

(e) ____________

(f) ____________

(g) ____________

(h) ____________

Vertebrates or Invertebrates

The five most well known classes of vertebrates (animals with backbones) are mammals, birds, fish, reptiles, amphibians. Invertebrates are animals which don't have a skeleton. For example insects, spiders, snails.

Tick all the vertebrates

Flying south for the winter

You might have heard the term 'flying south for the winter.' The term refers to the practice where birds fly across vast distances to avoid the cold, harsh winter. Birds migrate south for the winter every year and will return to where they were born once the cold passes and food is readily available once more. Migration is when an animal moves from region or habitat to another during a particular season. Birds migrate twice a year, in order to find food, breed, grow or to find a better climate. Birds migrate to places which are warm, have an adequate food supply and are safe for breeding. Even birds that do not fly can migrate, such as penguins that migrate by swimming.

Unlike other animals, birds are unable to build nests that would ensure that they would survive the winter. Therefore many birds will migrate half-way across the world to search for warm climates to spend the winter months. Birds don't change the places they migrate to every year. They follow patterns of movement that have remained unchanged for generations.

Which Bird will reach First

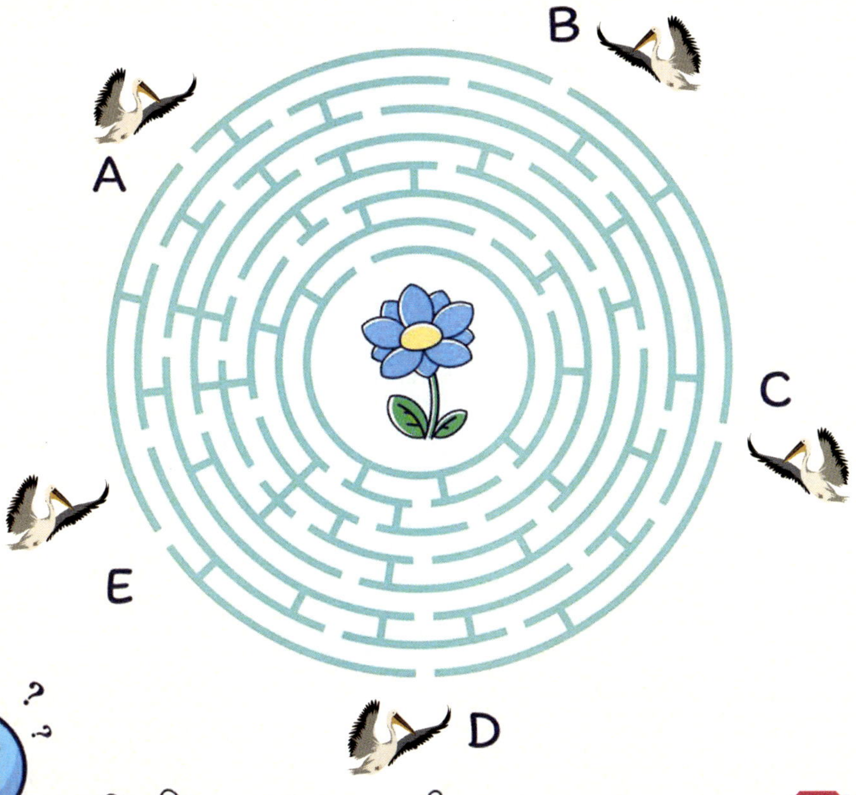

Ape or Monkey?

Apes are the animals that are most closely related to humans. Both apes and humans are members of the scientific group of animals called primates. Monkeys are primates, too. However, apes differ from monkeys in several ways. For instance, apes have more complex brains than monkeys do. Also, monkeys have tails but apes do not.

The apes are divided into two categories: great apes and lesser apes. Gorillas, orangutans, chimpanzees, and bonobos are great apes. They are larger and more intelligent than the lesser apes. The gibbons are lesser apes.

Apes live in warm or hot rainforests. Gibbons and orangutans are found in southeastern Asia. Gorillas and chimpanzees are found in western and central Africa. Bonobos have the smallest range. They are found only in part of the Democratic Republic of the Congo, a country in central Africa. Gibbons and orangutans live mainly in trees. On the other hand, gorillas spend most of their time on the ground. Chimpanzees and bonobos tend to eat and sleep in trees, but they travel mostly on the ground.

Colour it

Moth or a Butterfly?

Butterflies and moths are related kinds of flying insects. The adults develop from an immature form called a caterpillar. There are about 100,000 species, or types, of butterflies and moths. They live in many different habitats nearly all over the world.

Butterflies and moths have many features in common. Like all insects, they have six legs. Most adults have two pairs of wings. Dustlike scales cover the wings, body, and legs.

There are several differences, however, between butterflies and moths. Butterfly antennas, or feelers, are slender and end in little knobs.

Moth antennas lack these knobs. They often look like tiny feathers or threads. In addition, butterfly wings are usually brightly colored or boldly patterned. Most moths have a duller color and a thicker body than butterflies do.

How Do Caterpillars Turn into butterflies?

As children, many of us learn about the wondrous process by which a caterpillar morphs into a butterfly. The story usually begins with a very hungry caterpillar hatching from an egg. The caterpillar, or what is more scientifically termed a larva, stuffs itself with leaves, growing plumper and longer through a series of molts in which it sheds its skin. One day, the caterpillar stops eating, hangs upside down from a twig or leaf and spins itself a silky cocoon or molts into a shiny chrysalis. Within its protective casing, the caterpillar radically transforms its body, eventually emerging as a butterfly or moth.

Putting the Earth in Science

Rocks and minerals! Volcanoes! Weather and oceans! And so much more. Earth is a gigantic laboratory. All types of scientists work every day trying to understand our planet.

They love Earth Science. Earth Science is, well, you guessed it, the study of the Earth. Some scientists are geologists. They study rocks, minerals, and lots of other things like volcanoes, earthquakes, and floods.

When it is going to rain or snow, be sunny or stormy, ask a meteorologist. They study Earth's atmosphere and how climate changes over time. If a volcano blows its top, volcanologist find out what's going on. Oceanographers study all the different layers of the ocean and the organisms that live there.

Earth is made up of four major layers.
Do you know what they are?

The outermost layer is the CRUST. We live on the crust.
Under the crust is the MANTLE.
The next layer is the OUTER CORE. The outer core is liquid.
The INNER CORE is solid. Label each of the different layers.

Label each of the different layers

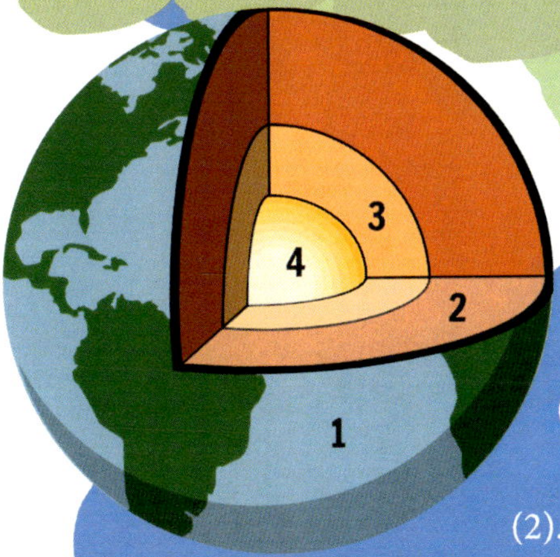

(1)..

(2)..

(3)..

(4)..

Rock On!

Rocks are everywhere. They can be as small as a pebble or as large as a mountain. Each type of rock is formed in a different way. In fact, you can tell rocks apart by looking at their colour, texture, and the minerals they are made from. Minerals are natural ingredients of rocks. Sometimes they are so small you can't even see them.

Rocks fall into three groups depending on the way they are formed. Some are igneous. Igneous means "from fire." Igneous rocks are formed deep below the ground where it is scalding hot. Sedimentary rock are formed over millions of years from dirt, silt and other things that settle on the bottoms of rivers, lakes and oceans.

Metamorphic rock changes over time by heat and pressure. Igneous and sedimentary rocks can change into metamorphic rock. Slate, for example, was once shale, a sedimentary rock.

colour it

Volcano

A volcano is an opening in Earth's crust. When a volcano erupts, hot gases and melted rock from deep within Earth find their way up to the surface. This material may flow slowly out of a fissure, or crack, in the ground, or it may explode suddenly into the air. Volcanic eruptions may be very destructive. But they also create new landforms. There are more than 1,500 potentially active volcanoes in the world today.

During a volcanic eruption, hot melted rock called magma escapes from a vent, or opening, in Earth's surface, or crust. Magma released from a volcano is known as lava.

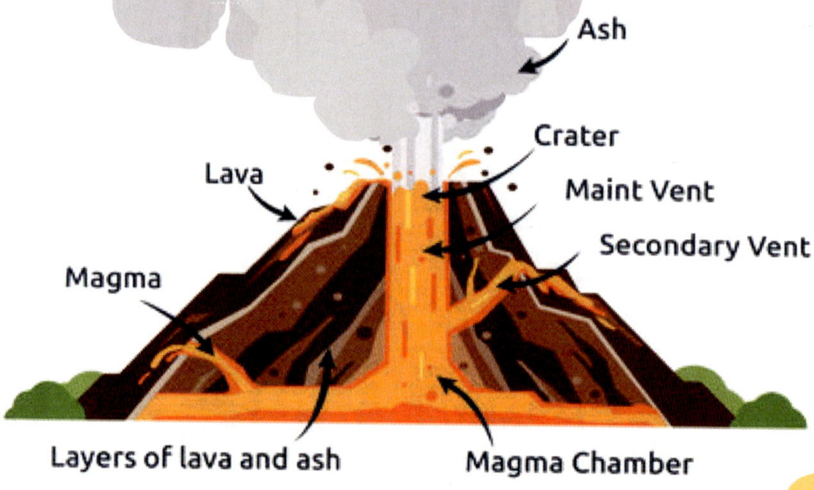

Earth's crust is made up of huge, rocky pieces called plates. The plates move slowly over the crust. Most volcanoes lie along the boundaries between these plates.

Find a safe place

Earthquake!!!

Imagine you're holding a rubber band and you suddenly pull it really hard in one direction, then let go. What happens? The rubber band shakes and ripples, right? Earthquakes are kind of like that, but on a much bigger scale! Earthquakes happen when two large pieces of the Earth's crust suddenly slip. This causes shock waves to shake the surface of the Earth in the form of an earthquake.

Where do earthquakes happen?

Earthquakes usually occur on the edges of large sections of the Earth's crust called tectonic plates. These plates slowly move over a long period of time. Sometimes the edges, which are called fault lines, can get stuck, but the plates keep moving. Pressure slowly starts to build up where the edges

are stuck and, once the pressure gets strong enough, the plates will suddenly move causing an earthquake.
Scientists record the shock waves produced in an earthquake with an instrument called a seismograph.

Earthquake Rebus!

A rebus is a puzzle where words are represented by a combination of letters and pictures. The key to figuring out a rebus is to look closely at the location of the letters and words, and put them together.

1

The ll=il+d + -K S+

2

mo+ b=v -s + -ud My

3

The +s -ir +ell

4

+'s +ed

What about Weather?

Weather is all around us, and it's basically what's happening outside. The way the air and the atmosphere feels is called weather. It's what you feel when you step out of your house, whether it's sunny, rainy, windy, or snowy. Weather can change from day to day and even throughout the day. Weather includes the temperature, wind strength, rain, sun, hail, fog, cloud etc.

Weather is studied by scientists called meteorologists who use special tools like thermometers, barometers, anemometers, and satellites to understand and predict what the weather will be like. It's always good to pay attention to the weather forecast, especially if you're planning to go outside or if there's a big event happening.

Crossword Weather Report

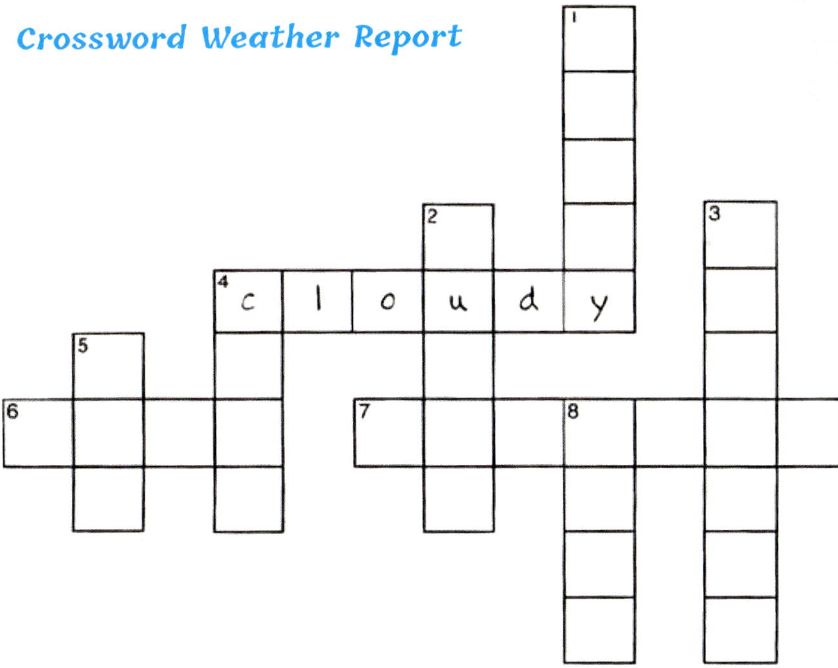

Across →

4 

6 

7 

Down ↓

1 

2 

3 

4 

5 

8 

Cyclone

A tropical cyclone is a circular storm that forms over warm oceans. When a tropical cyclone hits land, it brings heavy rains and strong winds. The winds can destroy buildings and rip out trees by their roots.

Tropical cyclones have different names around the world. Those that form near North America and the Caribbean are called hurricanes. Those that form near the Philippines, Japan, and China are known as typhoons. Those near Australia and in the Indian Ocean are often called cyclones.

Scientists use satellites and airplanes to track tropical storms. They watch closely to see if they develop into cyclones. They warn people that a hurricane may hit the coast. People may need to board up their windows and seek shelter away from the storm.

Hurricane Word Search

h	l	d	o	p	y	b	z	e	n	j	g	e	I	d
z	z	a	x	I	w	R	n	R	a	I	n	y	I	o
w	n	x	n	I	b	a	R	o	m	e	t	e	R	o
a	t	I	u	d	c	p	l	R	d	b	w	q	f	l
h	e	x	d	I	f	u	l	l	l	e	n	n	u	f
e	a	n	R	m	k	a	x	c	l	t	I	R	k	e
o	I	R	x	e	c	c	l	y	l	a	d	s	v	s
w	u	t	b	a	k	m	a	l	n	t	e	t	v	t
h	z	f	a	s	n	z	s	a	g	u	j	z	l	t
I	t	f	d	u	g	I	t	y	t	b	b	R	k	c
f	k	s	a	R	m	u	I	u	m	w	j	a	f	u
m	q	x	k	e	R	R	v	c	y	b	w	j	m	v
n	n	x	d	e	a	a	o	R	I	q	a	d	o	z
x	c	h	g	a	c	k	y	t	a	f	d	t	w	e
y	q	R	n	q	I	l	g	b	s	v	z	j	l	m

BAROMETER	HURRICANE	RAIN
EYE	LANDFALL	STORM
FLOOD	MEASURE	WALL
FUNNEL	NATURE	WIND

Drought

Drought is when there isn't enough rain for a really long time. Imagine if you were waiting for rain to water your plants, but it just didn't come for weeks or even months. That's what happens during a drought. It makes the land very dry, and plants and animals can't get enough water to survive. So, drought is like when nature forgets to give us the water we need. It's not good because it can make it hard for plants to grow, animals to find water, and even for people to have enough water for their homes.

Bingo!

Look around you then try to spot the following. Lets see if you can bingo on this one.

B	I	N	G	O
Dead plant on a vase	Today is sunny day	Lemonade	Stream	Dripping water
Healthy soil	Grassland	Water sprinkler	Electric fan	Wet socks
Air conditioner	A person drinking water		Watering can	Drinking fountain
Yellow leaves	Sands	Ice water	Dry and cracked land	Pool
Rain catch system	Ice cream	Yellow grass	A water jug	Today is a rainy day.

Weather Forecast

A weather forecast is like a prediction about what the weather is going to be like in the future. It's like when you try to guess what game your friend will want to play tomorrow. But instead of games, it's about guessing if it will be sunny, rainy, windy, or snowy outside.

People who study the weather, called meteorologists, use special tools and computers to help them make these predictions. They look at things like temperature, air pressure, clouds, and wind to figure

out what the weather might be. Then, they tell us about it on TV, the internet, or in the newspaper.

So, a weather forecast is like a smart guess about what the weather will be like tomorrow or in the next few days, so we can be prepared and plan our day accordingly!

Match the weather to the correct picture

Dinosaurs

Dinosaurs were the main animals on Earth for more than 150 million years. They were lizardlike reptiles. Some of them were the largest and scariest creatures that ever walked on land. Dinosaurs were different sizes. Some dinosaurs were smaller than a chicken. Others weighed as much as 100 tons—more than 10 times as much as the largest elephants. Dinosaurs did not have any hair. Their skin had a bumpy or pebbly surface.

The last dinosaurs became extinct, or died out, about 65.5 million years ago. Fossils of dinosaurs were first discovered in the early 1800s. Fossils are remains or impressions of a

plant or animal that have been preserved in rock. By studying these fossils, scientists know that dinosaurs were the ancient cousins of today's crocodiles, snakes, and lizards. Scientists also believe that today's birds descended from dinosaurs.

Match the Dinosaur Shadows

Our Neighbours

The solar system consists of the Sun and everything that orbits, or travels around, the Sun. This includes the eight planets and their moons, dwarf planets, and countless asteroids, comets, and other small, icy objects. However, even with all these things, most of the solar system is empty space.

The solar system itself is only a small part of a huge system of stars and other objects called the Milky Way galaxy. The solar system orbits around the center of the galaxy about once every 225 million years. The Milky Way galaxy is just one of billions of galaxies that in turn make up the universe.

COLOUR IT

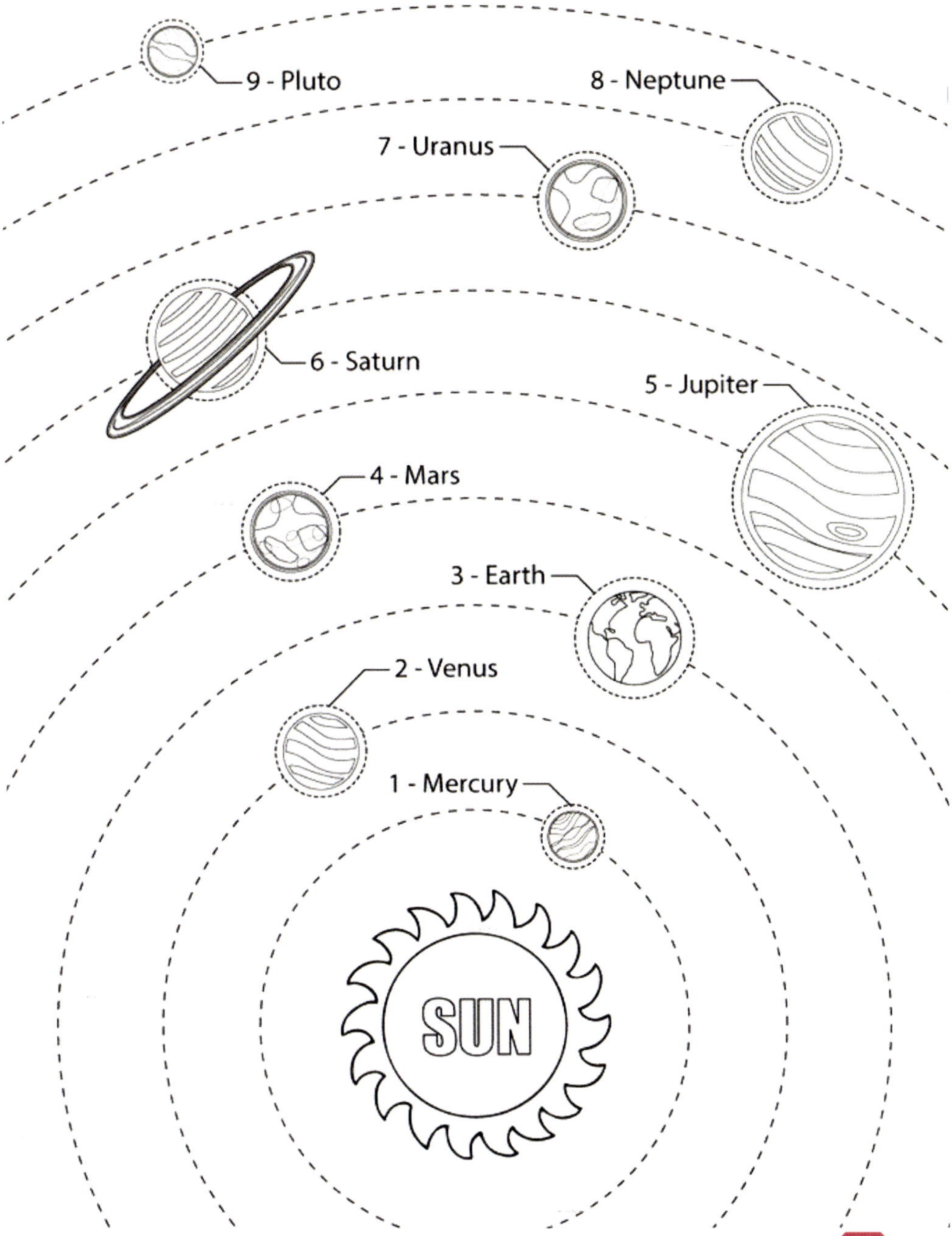
9 - Pluto
8 - Neptune
7 - Uranus
6 - Saturn
5 - Jupiter
4 - Mars
3 - Earth
2 - Venus
1 - Mercury
SUN

The Moon

The Moon is a large natural object that orbits, or travels around, Earth. After the Sun it is the brightest object in the sky.

The average distance between the Moon and Earth is about 238,900 miles (384,400 kilometers). Compared to the distance between other planets and Earth, this distance is small. In fact, the Moon is close enough to affect the level of seas on Earth. Every day the seas seem to rise and fall. This is because of a force called gravity. The Moon's gravity pulls on Earth. It is too weak to affect the whole planet, but it does make the water move. This creates tides.

The phases of the Moon

The phases of the Moon are the different ways the Moon looks from Earth over the time of about a month. The Moon does not change shape. It just looks like it does because a different amount of the Sun reflects off it each day. As the Moon orbits the Earth, the part of the Moon that faces the Sun will be lit up. When the Moon looks like it is getting larger, it is called waxing. When the Moon looks like it is getting smaller, it is called waning. Each phase repeats itself every 29.5 days.

Colour the moon phases

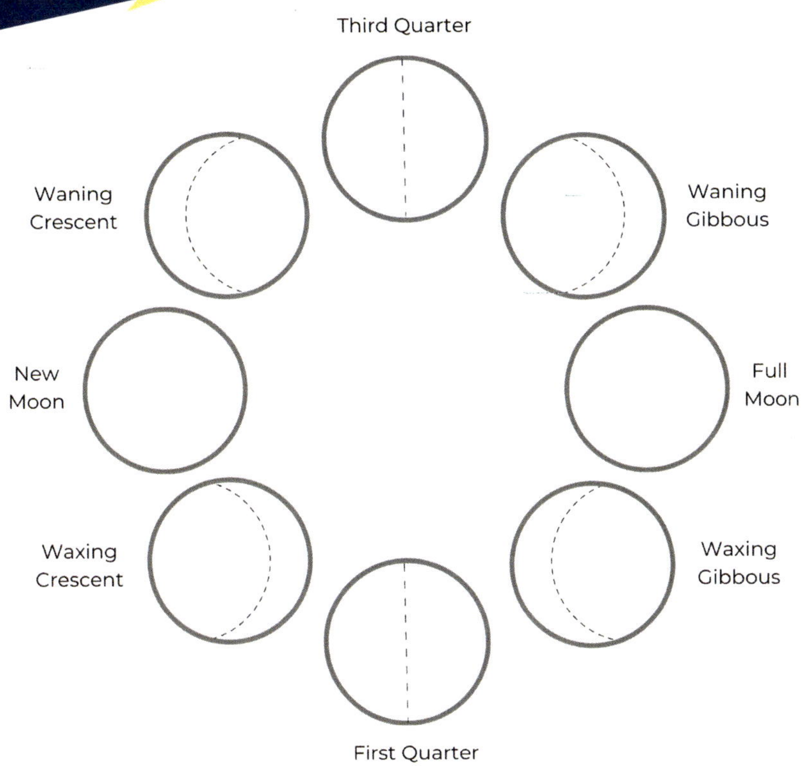

The Sun

A star is a hot, glowing ball of gas. When you look up in the night sky, you can see countless twinkling stars. Can you see any stars during the daytime? Of course! The light of daytime comes from our closest star: the Sun.

Just how close is the Sun to Earth? Way, way closer than other stars, but still pretty far away. It's approximately 93 million miles away from Earth. That's 400 times farther than the distance between Earth and the Moon!

However, it's a good thing that Earth isn't too close to the Sun. If we were too close, it would be way too hot to live here. The Sun's surface is very hot, and its atmosphere is even hotter. And the Sun's core is the hottest part of all, at a sizzling 27 million degrees Fahrenheit!

Our Sun is about 100 times wider than Earth, but it is just an average sized star. Astronomers have found some stars that are 100 times bigger than the Sun and others that are 10 times smaller.

Puzzle

Comets vs. Asteroids

Comets

Comets are large objects made of dust and ice that orbit the Sun. Best known for their long, streaming tails, these ancient objects are leftovers from the formation of the solar system 4.6 billion years ago.

The gravity of a planet or star can pull comets from their homes in the Kuiper Belt or Oort Cloud. This tug can redirect a comet toward the Sun. The paths of these redirected comets look like long, stretched ovals.

Why do comets have tails?

As dust and gases stream away from the nucleus, sunlight and particles coming from the Sun push them into a bright tail that stretches behind the comet for millions of miles.

Asteroids

Asteroids are small, rocky bodies that orbit, or travel around, the sun. They are also called minor planets or planetoids. In general, they are materials left over from when the planets formed. They are also created when other bodies in space collide and break apart. Most asteroids travel around the sun in a loose path that falls between the orbits of the planets Mars and Jupiter.

Asteroids are much smaller than planets. Many small asteroids enter Earth's atmosphere each day. Almost all burn up before they hit the ground. As they burn they create a streak of light called a meteor. An asteroid that survives the fall through the atmosphere and reaches Earth's surface is called a meteorite.

What's the Matter?

Look around you. What do you see? Lots of stuff, right? A light. A book. A computer. A glass of water. Maybe there is a hot cup of steaming tea nearby. All of these things are different. Yet, they are all the same. Each is an example of matter.

Matter is anything that takes up space and has mass. Mass is the amount of matter in an object. You notice mass by how much an object weighs. Everything you see, smell, or touch, and even things you cannot see, smell, or touch, are all examples of matter.

Forms of the Matter

Matter comes in three forms: solids, like a book; liquids, like water; and gas, like air. Each form of matter is made up of very small particles called molecules. Molecules are so small that you can't even see them under a microscope. In a solid object, like a table, molecules are packed very close together. In a liquid, like a glass of cranberry juice, molecules are farther apart. In a gas, like the air inside a balloon, the molecules move fast, bouncing off one another.

Matter can change from one state to another. An ice cube, for example, is a solid. When it melts, it turns into a liquid-water. If you heat water, it turns into a gas-steam.

Label each state of matter. Write **solid, liquid** or **gas**.

(a) ______________ (b) ______________ (c) ______________

Observing changes in matter. Drag the correct answer to the line.

(a)  ______________ gas to liquid

(b)  ______________ liquid to gas

(c)  ______________ solid to liquid

Energy

Everything on the planet runs on energy. You, your dog, even the waves on the ocean. Energy is the ability to do work or cause change.

There are two kinds of energy: kinetic and potential. Kinetic energy is the energy of movement. A moving school bus has kinetic energy. Potential energy is stored energy. A book sitting on a table is packed with stored energy. That means it has the potential to do work.

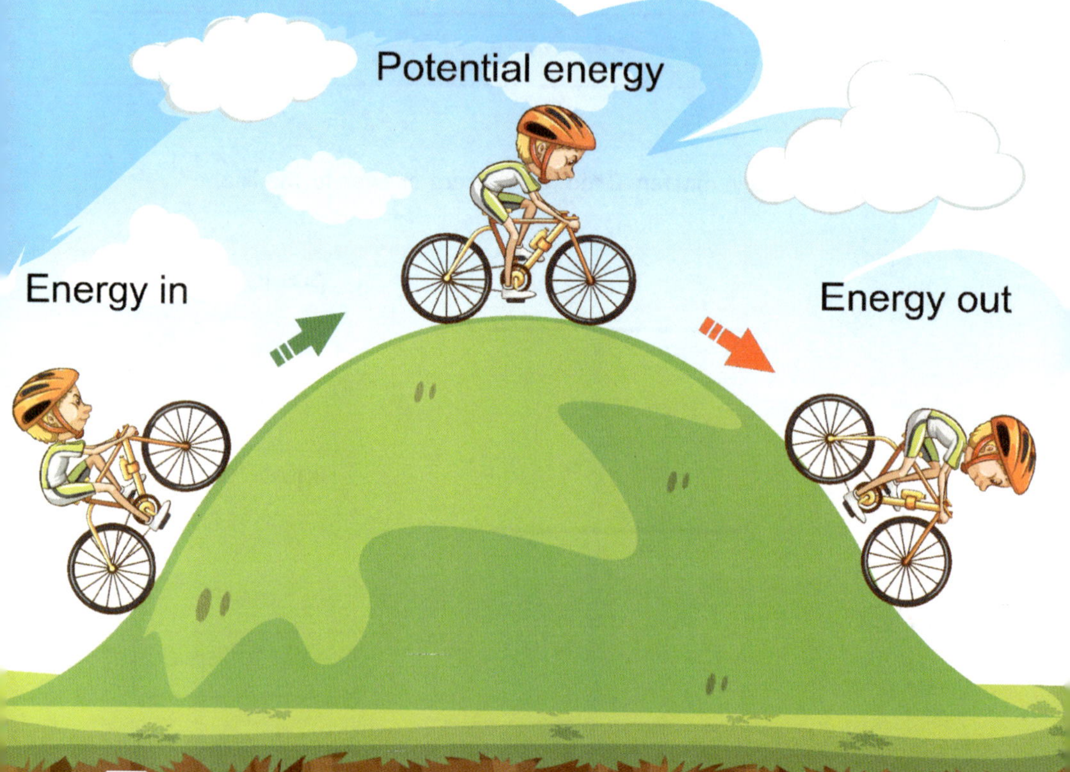

Energy comes in different forms. Mechanical energy is a type of kinetic energy. It is energy associated with the motion or position of an object.

A grasshopper leaping is a form of mechanical energy, as is the school bus you ride in.

Thermal energy is heat energy, a form of kinetic energy. That's because the total energy of the particles in an object are moving so fast that it feels warm to the touch. Melting icecream is an example of what happens when thermal energy rises.

Chemical energy is potential energy stored in the bonds that hold chemical compounds together.

Kinetic or Potential?

- ☐ PE
- ☐ KE
- ☐ both
- ☐ unsure

(a)

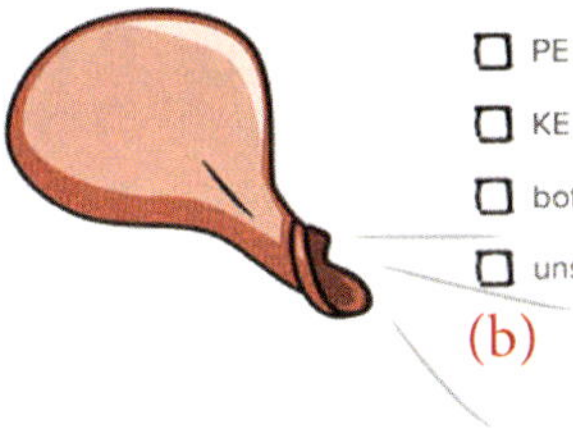

- ☐ PE
- ☐ KE
- ☐ both
- ☐ unsure

(b)

- ☐ PE
- ☐ KE
- ☐ both
- ☐ unsure

(c)

- ☐ PE
- ☐ KE
- ☐ both
- ☐ unsure

(d)

- ☐ PE
- ☐ KE
- ☐ both
- ☐ unsure

(e)

- ☐ PE
- ☐ KE
- ☐ both
- ☐ unsure

(f)

STEAM

TECHNOLOGY

Technology - An Important Part of Our Life

From the television you watch to the mobile phone you use to connect with your near and dear ones, from the car you drive to the refrigerator you use to store your food, from the air conditioners you use to beat the heat to the laptops yop use to accomplish various - tasks-everything is a gift to technology.

Let's look at the following picture of technologies inventions that have made living convenient.

Write their names under the picture.

In the House

There are a wide variety of household gadgets in use today, and new ones are always being developed and incorporated into homes. The genreral purpose of most gadgets is to make life easier, mor fun, or more efficient. It helps with household chores, including cooking, cleaning, and food preservation too.

GADGETS

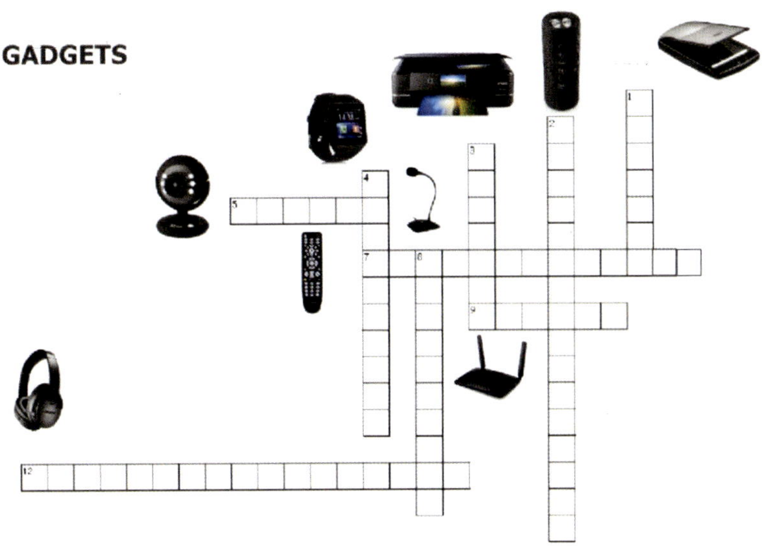

Braile Machines

Technology has made is possible for blind people to read. A Braille machine, also known as a Braille typewriter or Braille embosser, is a device used to create documents in Braille, a tactile writing system used by people who are blind or visually impaired. Braille allows individuals to read and write using raised dots arranged in specific patterns, representing letters, numbers, punctuation marks, and even musical notation.

Louis's Story

Louis Braille was a smart boy who lost his sight when he was very young. He went to a special school for blind children in Paris, where he felt frustrated with the books they had. So, he created a new way for blind people to read and write using raised dots. This became known as Braille. Louis Braille's system made life easier for blind people all over the world

Braille Riddles Deciphered!

Given below is the braille alphabet.

Can you solve these riddles using the braille alphabet?

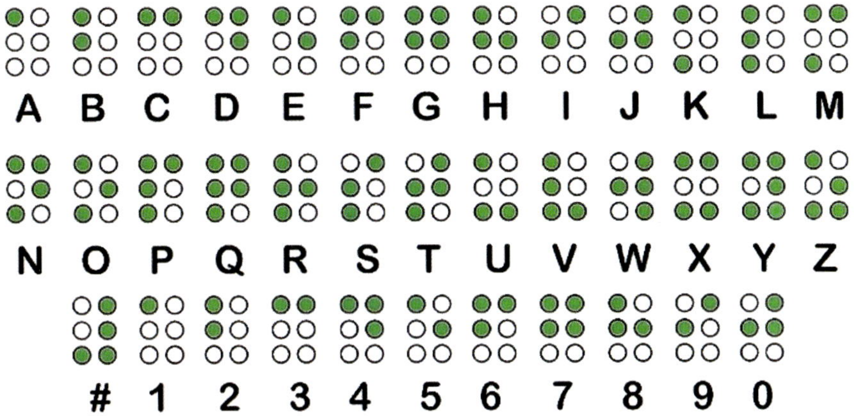

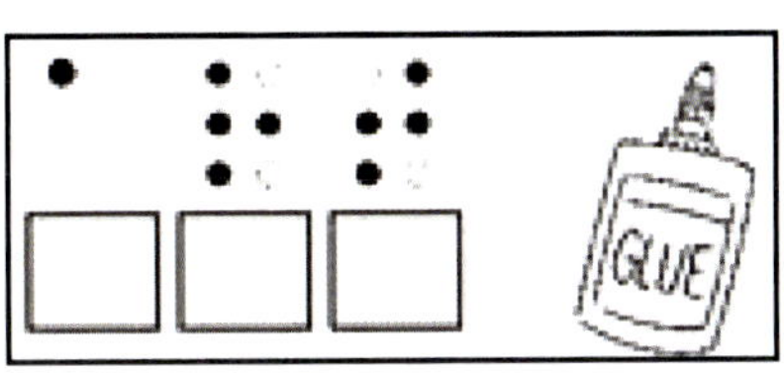

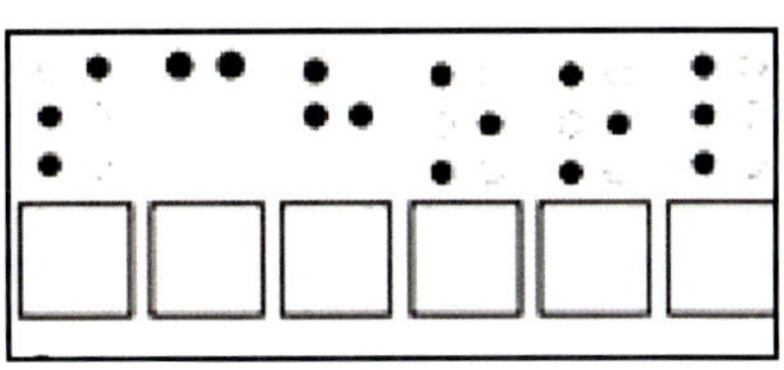

Are you Space Explorer?

Through space exploration humans have learned a great deal about the planets, stars, and other objects in space. More than 5,000 spacecraft have been launched into space to gather information since 1957. They include spacecraft with humans on board, space probes, and satellites.

The Soviet Union (now Russia) and the United States were originally the main countries exploring space. Many other countries are now involved. Astronauts also must improve their physical fitness. They make special trips in airplanes to get used to the feeling of weightlessness. Humans cannot survive in outer space on their own.

The environment is not the same as it is on Earth. Astronauts therefore travel in space in tightly sealed compartments. They bring their own supply of oxygen with them.

Find objects in the puzzle and discover the hidden word

ASTRONAUT
SATELLITE
STAR
ALIEN
UFO
PLANET
ROCKET

A	S	T	U	S	★	R
S	S	R	P	F	A	O
T	A	O	N	P	O	C
A	T	E	A	L	A	K
R	C	L	U	T	N	E
A	★	L	I	T	E	T
L	I	E	N	E	T	E

Robot

A robot is a machine that does tasks without the help of a person. Many people think of robots as machines that look and act like people. Most robots, though, do not look like people. And robots do only what a person has built them to do.

Robots are especially useful because they can do things that could be dangerous for people. For example, they can be sent deep underwater or into space.

Wings of the Future

On December 17, 1903, the first mechanical airplane took off. The world changed in an instant. The plane was built by two brothersn- Orville and Wilbur Wright. It was made out of fabric and wood. The flight lasted only 12 seconds. The plance travelled 120 feed. The flight was short but amazing. No one had flown in a motorized aircraft before.

Over the years, engineers and scientists have made the Wright brother's invention faster, sleeker and more powerful. We now have jets that can fly faster than the speed of sound. The Wright brothers would love the airplanes of the future. Many will make flying easier and faster. While one may flap its wings, the others will make as little noise as possible.

Help the plane fly to the Island

Helicopter

A helicopter is a kind of aircraft. Unlike an airplane, a helicopter can fly straight up and down, sideways, or backward. It can also spin around or hover motionless in the air. Helicopters can fly lower than airplanes can, too. A helicopter's wings are thin, narrow blades that rotate, or spin around. The blades on top of a helicopter, along with the parts that connect them, are called the main rotor. The main rotor is connected to an engine. The engine sends power to the main rotor to spin the blades. As the blades spin, air pushes against them. Helicopters are useful because they can fly almost anywhere.

Connect the dots and colour it.

Remote control

I was completely mesmerised with how a lump of plastic could possibly change channels on a TV without any physical connection.

Very early TV remote controls worked with wires. Then we created battery-powered remotes and we didn't need the wires any more.

Now remotes are everywhere. In fact, the planet-watching Voyager spacecraft are controlled remotely and they are presently 20 billion kilometres away. It takes 20 hours for instructions to travel from Earth to the spacecraft but we can do it – using a remote.

Did you know, in a remote-controlled toy car, radio waves must be emitted by its remote control whereas in the television remote, emission of infrared waves takes place. Sir Nikola Tesla invented the remote control system in the 1800s.

Quiz:

Q.1 Remote controls are ____ objects.

1. Wireless.
2. Wired.
3. Both (1) and (2).
4. None of the above.

Q.2 ____ is sent as a signal to convey our actions to another device.

1. Waves.
2. Lines.
3. Dots.
4. Sound.

Q.3. ___ are transmitted by the remote of remote-controlled toy.

1. Radio waves.
2. Infrared waves.
3. X-ray waves.
4. None of the above.

Home on Mars

A Mars habitat is a hypothetical place where humans could live on Mars. Mars habitats would have to contend with surface conditions that include almost no oxygen in the air, extreme cold, low pressure, and high radiation. Alternatively, the habitat might be placed underground, which helps solve some problems but creates new difficulties.

One challenge is the extreme cost of transporting building materials to the Martian surface. So, scientists propose the possibility of using materials from Mars to construct homes. While the gravity on Mars is lower than that on Earth, there are stronger solar radiation and temperature cycles, and high internal forces needed for pressurized habitats to contain air.

Growing food on Mars won't look like the farms that we have on Earth. Instead, crops would need to be grown without soil, such as tank farming or aquaculture. This is where the food would be planted in nutrient-rich water and fed with artificial lights.

Find 10 differences

Rise of the Drones

What to you get when you cross a robot with a remote-controlled toy? Give up? You get a drone. Drones are aircraft whose flight is controlled from the ground. Drones can do all sorts of things. Some drones are high-flying weapons. The military uses them. Some drones are television cameras. Television stations use them to give viewers a bird's eye view of a news event.

The world of drones is getting larger by the day. Farmers will one day use camera-crarryng drones to find crop-eating insects. Some companies plan to use drones to deliver pakagers.

Radar

A radar system is made up of a transmitter, a receiver, an antenna, and a display. The transmitter creates radio waves, which are invisible streams of energy. The antenna sends the waves out into the air. When the waves hit an object, they reflect, or bounce back, to the antenna. The waves then pass to the receiver, which makes sense of them. By measuring how long it takes the waves to return, the receiver can tell how far away the object is. The receiver can also tell where a moving object is headed and at what speed. Sometimes it can tell how big the object is, too. The receiver sends this information to a display, or screen, for people to see. Radar is very useful. At airports, air-traffic controllers use radar to keep track of airplanes and direct their movements.

Connect the dots & colour

Text to Talk

When you wanted to say something to someone in the olden days, you had to speak to them face-to-face or write them letter.

Then, technology took over. People could talk over the phone. Then, Matti Makkone came along.

Makkone was a scientist from Finland who sent the first text message on December 3, 1992 Actually, he invented the SMS, which mea[n] Short Message Service.

The SMS allowed people to send electronic message, such as words and numbers, between two or more users.

With new technology of instant messaging applications people can now send digital images, such as photos, sound files, video files and yes, even emojis.

SECRET CODE

In Moroni 9:4 we are told that we can know the things written in the Book of Mormon are true. To know for ourselves Moroni says we have to pray and ask with what? Then the Holy Ghost will manifest the truth of it unto you.

CODE BOX

1	2	3	4	5	6	7	8	9	10	11	12	13	14	15	16	17	18
C	F	A	S	E	T	G	M	I	V	N	W	Y	H	R	L	D	O

__
3

__ __ __ __ __ __ __
4 9 11 1 5 15 5

__ __ __ __ __
14 5 3 15 6

__ __ __ __
12 9 6 14

__ __ __ __
15 5 3 16

__ __ __ __ __ __
9 11 6 5 11 6

__ __ __ __ __ __
14 3 10 9 11 7

__ __ __ __ __
2 3 9 6 14

__ __
9 11

__ __ __ __ __ __
1 14 15 9 4 6

DNA Adventure

Imagine you're a brave explorer on a quest to uncover the secrets of life itself! Your journey begins with something very special: a tiny, invisible map hidden inside every living thing, including you! This map is called DNA.

Now, to read this magical map, you need a special tool - a DNA decoder! It's like having a super cool magnifying glass that can see inside your cells.

First, you collect a tiny sample of DNA, like a drop of magic potion from a wizard's cauldron. This could be a bit of saliva from your mouth, a piece of hair, or even a speck of dust. Then, you place it under the DNA decoder, and the adventure begins!

As you peer through the decoder, you see a world of letters, but not just any letters - these are the secret codes of DNA! And they hold the key to unlocking the mysteries of life.

You can follow the twists and turns of the DNA map, uncovering its hidden treasures. You might discover where your ancestors came from, or find clues about your family's past. You might even uncover secrets about your health, like whether you have a superpower to fight off certain diseases!

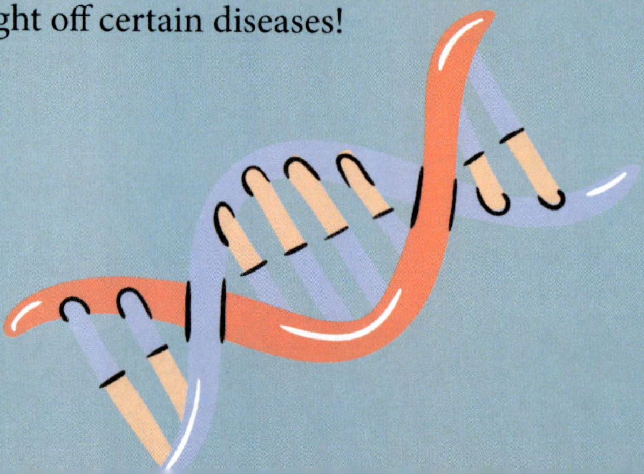

DNA THEMED WORD SEARCH

M A J F W H B P H E R S H E Y A Y C
C U D Q F T L A Y D N A P G J Y M H
P Y T E I W N G S R A L L E L E C R
H H T A N G P T E E I G G A A C H O
I G E O T O U R M N P M E J S N A M
P E C N S I S A O E O A I N U J S O
U N R U O I O I N T N T I D O H E S
R E I M O T N N N I E D Y R I M J O
I O C E T N Y E J E N I E P S N E M
N L K I H J O P Z N G E N L E F E E
E R J Z N U C L E O T I D E A Y T B
U T R R E P L I C A T I O N B W M U

REPLICATION
NUCLEOTIDE
PYRIMIDINE
CHROMOSOME
PHENOTYPE
ADENOSINE
BASEPAIRS
MUTATION

CYTOSINE
GENOTYPE
GUANINE
HERSHEY
PROTEIN
GENOME
ALLELE
MENDEL

PURINE
CRICK
CHASE
GENE
DNA

Solar Energy

Ancient Egyptians were the first people known to use the energy from sunlight to heat their homes. Fast forward to today, societies around the world have developed innovative technologies that allow us to turn the sun's energy into electricity that powers heating and cooling systems, transportation, lighting, and ventilation, just to name a few.

Solar power is a valuable energy source that can be used to heat buildings and produce electricity. It is the most abundant, fastest, and cheapest energy source on earth, and it generates minimal greenhouse gas emissions.

What is Solar Energy and How Does It Work?

Humans install solar panels in places where they are mostly exposed to the sunlight, for example on the roof of a house. The sun shines directly on so-called photovoltaic (PV) panels, which contain cells that can capture the sunlight's energy. This energy generates electrical charges that move around the cells, causing electricity to flow.

Colour it

Wind Energy

Wind power is an alternative energy source. This means that the power of the wind can be used in place of other energy sources such as coal, oil, and nuclear reactions. Wind can be used to produce electricity that heats homes and lights streets and buildings.

Wind power is harnessed by a machine called a wind turbine. Wind turbines are tall towers topped with blades. The blades are connected to a vertical shaft, or rod. When wind causes the blades to spin, they turn the shaft. The turning shaft provides power to a machine called a generator, which produces electricity.

A group of wind turbines, called a wind farm, can be used to provide electricity to a community. Small turbines provide power for individual homes.

Wind turbines used to be called windmills. The earliest-known windmills were built more than 1,000 years ago. People used them to grind grain. The Dutch used windmills to pump water out of low-lying areas near the sea.

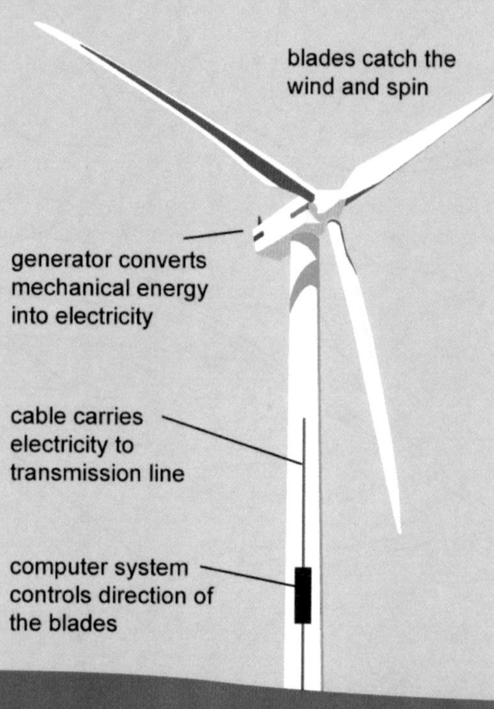

Connect the dots & colour.

Tidal Energy

Energy is everywhere. It's in the Sunlight. It's in the wind. It's in the ocean. The ocean has heat energy from soaking up the light energy of the Sun. And, like the wind, the ocean has energy of motion in the form of waves and currents. Tidal energy systems can extract either kinetic energy from the moving water of rivers, tides and open ocean currents; or potential energy from the difference in height between high and low tides. The first method - generating energy from tidal currents - is becoming more popular because people believe that it does not harm the environment as much as dams. Many coastal sites worldwide are being examined to see if they can be used to produce tidal energy. Like other hydroelectricity, tidal power produces no pollution and is a renewable energy source, because tides are caused by events that happen in the solar system and so will not run out. Tidal power has great potential for future power and electricity generation because of the very large amount of energy contained in these rotational systems.

House in the Space

A space station is a spacecraft in a fixed orbit around the Earth. Astronauts can live on a space station for days or months at a time while they gather scientific data and perform experiments. The first space station was Salyut 1, which was launched by the Soviet Union on April, 1971.

The space station is also a unique science laboratory. Several nations worked together to build and use the space station. The space station has the volume of a five-bedroom house or two Boeing 747 jetliners. It is able to support a crew of six people, plus visitors. Crews of seven people typically stay on the Space Station for about six months. They have electrical power provided by huge solar panels. However, they must bring or produce all of the air, water, and food that they need to survive. The air is carefully filtered to clean it. Water is recycled from the water vapor that crew members breathe out.

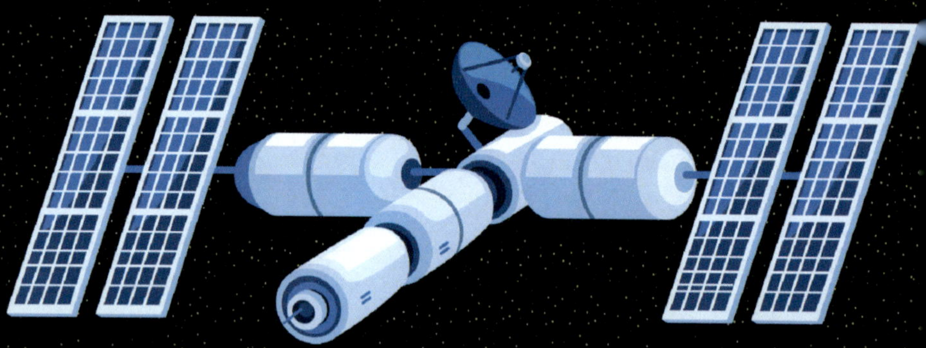

HELP THE ROCKET GET TO THE EARTH

Story of Internet

The Internet is a network, or system, that connects millions of computers worldwide.

Since its beginning, the Internet has changed a great deal. Advances in technology have made using the Internet quicker and easier. No longer limited to personal computers, the Internet can be accessed via tablet computers and most cell phones and televisions. As more and more people use the Internet, the quantity of information continues to grow. In the 1960s the U.S. government made a system that would let computers across the United States share information. By the mid-1970s many groups of computers were connected in networks. Machines called routers were invented to connect the networks. This is how the original ARPANET eventually grew into the Internet.

In 1989 hypertext was invented. Hypertext is a link between different parts of an electronic document or between different documents. Hypertext became the basis of the World Wide Web.

Help! I want my battery

It's All About Computers

When think about technology mostly first thing that comes in mind is the image of a compter. Computers are perhaps the best inventions made by man. Today, computer playes an important role in our lives and we are completely dependent on it. It is used in almost all fields, be it education or entertainment.

MONITOR

Displays information on a screen.

CASE

Contains the brains of your computer that processes information, including the central processing uniy (CPU) and other parts.

KEYBOARD

A device for typing letters, numbers and symblos into the compter.

MOUSE

A hand-held device for moving a cursor around the screen.

PRINTER

Put text and image from the computer onto paper.

MODEM / ROUTER

Sends a network signal to the computer; used to connect many computers to the network or the Internet.

Match the computer parts to the correct picture

Monitor

CPU

Keboard

Mouse

Self-Driving Car

A self-driving car, also known as an autonomous car. It is a car that is capable of traveling without human input. Self-driving cars use sensors to perceive their surroundings, such as optical and thermographic cameras, radar, GPS, odometry and inertial measurement units. Control systems interpret sensory information to create a three-dimensional model of the vehicle's surroundings. Based on the model, the car then identifies an appropriate navigation path and strategies for managing traffic controls and obstacles.

How long before we have Driverless Cars?

The concept of driverless cars was introduced to the world way back in 1939. Not surprisingly, Japan soon came up with an autonomous car that used cameras and analogue computing to process signals around 1977. Post that, the development of autonomous cars gained a footing in Europe in 1980s.

Since then, many major companies have entered the fray with model after model of driverless cars. With the advent of the Tesla Motor's and Google's autonomous cars however, the spotlight shining on this technology is brighter than ever.

Find the Route

STEAM

ENGINEERING

Simple Machine 1: The Inclined Plane

A machine is a thing that is created by people to make work easier. Some machines make moving or lifting things easier. The most basic machines are called simple machines. They are the inclined plane, the wedge, the lever, the wheel and axle, the screw, and the pulley.

Simple machines change the strength or direction of a force, such as a push or pull.

An inclined plane is a simple machine. It allows one to use less force to move an object. Examples of inclined planes are ramps, sloping roads and hills, plows, chisels, hatchets, carpenter's planes, and wedges.

Ramping it up

Circle all the examples of an inclined plane

(a)

(b)

(c)

(d)

(e)

Simple Machine 2: The Wedge

The wedge is basically a simple tool shaped like a triangle. It's thicker on one end and thinner on the other. You might see wedges used to split things apart, like a piece of wood. When you push the thin end of the wedge into something, it applies pressure and forces the object apart. Wedges work by changing direction and force. It's a simple but effective tool that's been used for thousands of years!

Which is a Wedge?

Which of the following are examples of wedges? Tick the correct box.

a

YES	NO

b

YES	NO

c

YES	NO

d

YES	NO

e

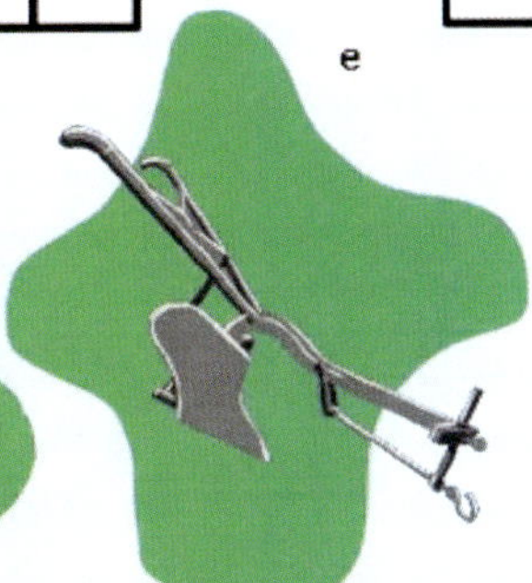

YES	NO

f

YES	NO

g

YES	NO

Lever is like a see-saw or a crowbar. It's a simple tool that helps you move things more easily. A lever has a pivot point, which is like the point in the middle of a see-saw where it balances. You apply force to one end of the lever, and it helps you move or lift something heavy on the other end.

Think of it like trying to lift a heavy rock. If you push down on a long stick (the lever) resting on a rock with a smaller end, the other end of the stick will rise, helping you lift the rock. It's all about using leverage to make lifting or moving things easier! Levers are used in many machines, like scissors, wheelbarrows, and even doors.

Simple Machine 3: The Lever

Find the Levers

Can you find all the different types of everyday levers in this word search?

O V W
X K H H A O F G F
W M S R Q M P R H I N P H
W I A S Q I X K Q R P B S O X J O
B U N D R S H U T A A O B O H J R L T
P U Y E S G X I B Q F B Y T O Q I W L M X
N S M R N W R U O V V L Y Z A T I N C W W
H Z P E O F S V I T S B E W C I V W P G V R M
G J Z T M T J S E T S R E I L P S A M W R Z C
B R E E J E Q A D E L H M H Q P H W R C R L O R Z
E E W S L N H A M M E R R W I E T P E F X N P D N
W A K T W B N X C F O W P L A X R X K P D E X E L
T J L C A M C Z Q V O P B E R B U J P S N W B P P B V
U T Q A P D C L I P P E R S R R L N N V Q K J I R F F
F K N M L W L R S L V N K J G K D N Q O Q K L C E O T
O S E E J G G O M Y E Q T I T U Z B D U I C X A R
T I D R A S I U S U R V A U T T N O W A H L W E J
W N E C N O C V X H N G V C U C R U N V T U U B M
V Y M I R O T I F M M R Z D E R P C X Q Z L Q
S R K D T G S I W W A V A P T K Q Q U S S H N
F O G E M T H O C I A V C M X P N C Z R U
X O S T B S W K T E D N W O I R I E P B W
C C R M L E A H E X I Y V Q S F I A V
D L Q R T E S E N V T D S G N N S
F J B B L E L T P O L H K
N A Q Y E T R D W
J G S

WHEELBARROW	PLIERS	HAMMER
FISHINGROD	TWEEZERS	EXCAVATOR
NAIL	CLIPPERS	SCISSORS
BOTTLEOPENER	SHEARS	TONGS
SEESAW	NUTCRACKER	STAPLER

Simple Machine 4: The Screw

Screw is like a twisty nail with ridges spiraling around it. When you turn a screw, it goes into something, like wood or metal, or it can come out. The ridges on the screw help it grip whatever it's going into.

Think of it like a staircase. When you walk up a staircase, you have to take steps one by one, right? Each step helps you go up. Well, the ridges on a screw work the same way. When you turn the screw, it moves up or down, depending on which way you turn it.

Screws are used in lots of things, like holding things together, like pieces of furniture, or in machines to help things move. They're handy little things!

Find the Screws

When completed, this grid will contain the names of six screws you might find around the house. Some of the words will interlock. Others will be diagonal. The only words that go in the puzzle are the ones in the word list. There are no spaces between compound words. Can you fill them in?

B			C			J		C				
												R
			T									
		G										L
												B
		T			E			P				
F		U										
									R			

Word List

Bolt	Carjack	Faucet	Lightbulb
Bottletop	Drillbit	Jarlid	

Simple Machine 5 : The Wheel and Axle

Imagine a wheel on a bike. Now, think about how the wheel connects to the bike. There's a rod, called an axle, that goes through the middle of the wheel. The wheel spins around this rod, allowing the bike to move smoothly.

Now, let's talk about how this works. The wheel and axle make things easier to move because they help to distribute force. When you push or pull on the wheel, the force you use gets spread out over the axle, making it easier to move something heavy.

You see, the wheel and axle are like a team. The wheel is the big, round part, and the axle is the rod in the middle. When they work together, they make moving things, like your bike, much easier!

Colour the Wheel

Simple Machine 6: Pulley

Let's imagine you have to lift a really heavy bucket of water from a well. It would be really hard to do it all by yourself, right? That's where a pulley comes in to help!

A pulley is like a simple machine that makes it easier to lift heavy things. It's made up of a wheel with a groove around its edge and a rope or a belt that goes around the wheel. When you pull one end of the rope, the wheel turns, and it helps you lift the heavy object.

Here's how it works: when you pull down on one end of the rope, the pulley lets you lift the heavy bucket by spreading the force you use to pull it up. So, instead of you having to lift the whole weight of the bucket by yourself, the pulley helps to share the load with you.

A **PULLEY** is a simple machine made with a wheel and a rope to lift objects.

Check the pictures that show how people use a pulley in their everyday life.

(a)

(b)

(c)

(d)

(e)

(f)

(g)

Energy

Energy is like the power that makes things happen. Everything around us needs energy to work. Imagine your favorite toy car zooming across the floor – it needs energy to move. Even your body needs energy to run, jump, and play! There are different types of energy. One kind is called "Kinetic Energy." This is the energy of things that are moving, like your toy car or when you kick a soccer ball.

Another type is "Potential Energy." This is energy that's stored and waiting to be used. For example, when you hold a ball up high before dropping it, it has potential energy because it's ready to fall and move.

Hydraulics

Hydraulics is like magic that helps big things move with ease! It's all about using water or oil to make stuff happen. Imagine squeezing a water balloon – the water inside pushes out and makes the balloon move. That's kind of how hydraulics work!

Here's the cool part: when you push down on a small tube filled with water or oil, it makes a big tube push up! This helps lift heavy things, like cars in a car repair shop or even big machines at construction sites.

Hydraulics are super important in our world because they make it easier for us to do lots of things, like lifting heavy stuff or stopping cars smoothly. So next time you see a big machine at work, remember that hydraulics are the secret behind its strength and power!

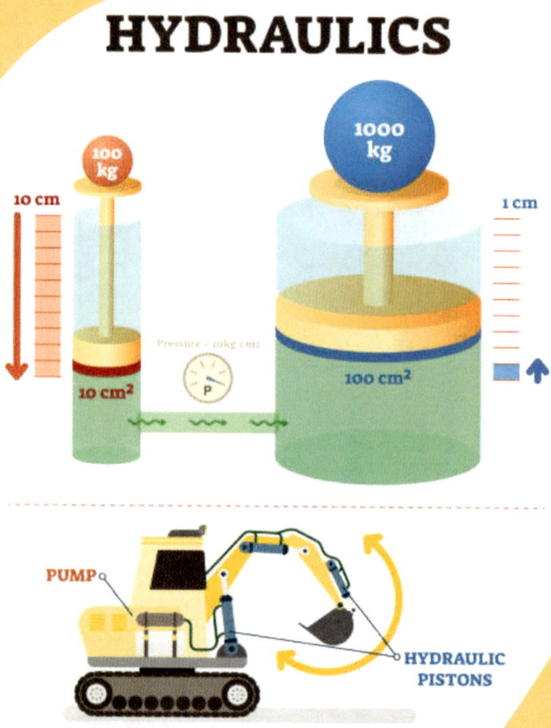

Can you find the path to the toothpaste

Dimples of a Golf Ball

When you look at a golf ball, you'll notice it has little dents or dimples all over its surface. These dimples might seem like they're just there for decoration, but they actually serve a very important purpose in the game of golf.

You see, when a golf ball is hit by a golf club, it goes flying through the air. But here's the interesting part: the dimples on the golf ball help it fly farther and more accurately.

When the golf ball is flying through the air, it creates an area of turbulence around it. This turbulence creates drag, which is like air resistance pushing against the ball. Without dimples, the air would stick to the ball's surface more, creating even more drag and making the ball slow down quickly.

However, the dimples on the golf ball disrupt the airflow around it. They create a thin layer of turbulent air called a boundary layer. This boundary layer helps reduce drag, allowing the ball to fly farther with less resistance.

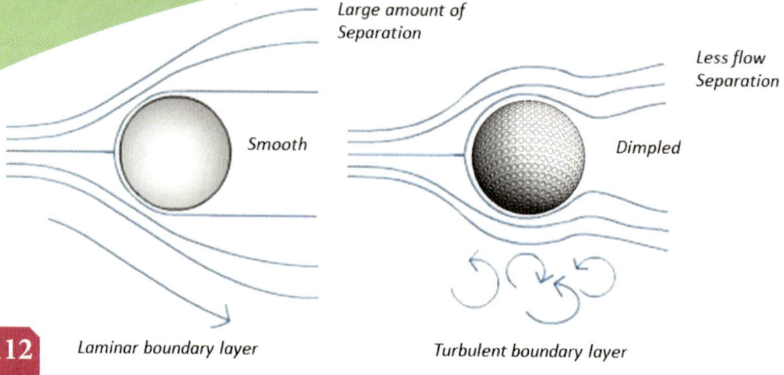

It's kind of like how the wings of an airplane are designed to reduce drag and make the plane more aerodynamic.

Find the path

Bridge: Road in The Sky

Imagine you're at one side of a big river, and your friend is on the other side. How do you both get to each other without swimming? That's where a bridge comes in! A bridge is like a giant pathway that helps people and cars cross over things like rivers, valleys, or even roads. It's like a road in the sky!

1. Beam Bridge: Look for images of simple bridges with a long horizontal beam supported by pillars or abutments at each end. They're often straightforward and common in many places.

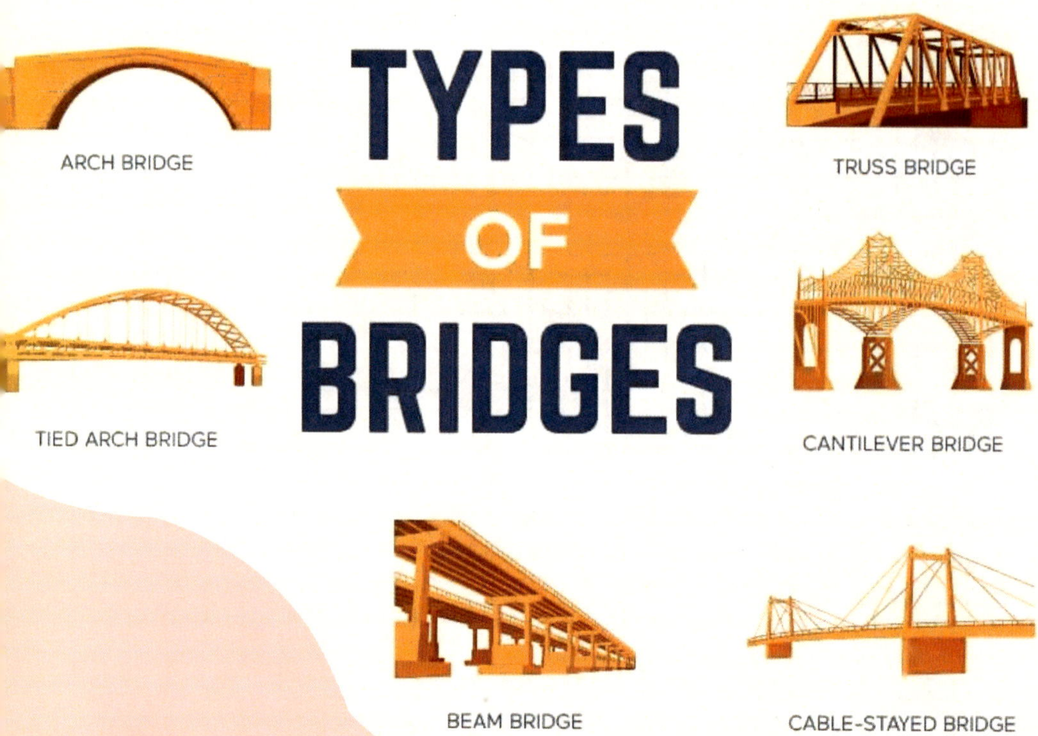

2. Arch Bridge: Search for images of bridges with a curved structure spanning the gap. You'll see the distinctive arch shape, which is usually made of stone, concrete, or steel.
3. Suspension Bridge: Find images of bridges with tall towers and cables stretching from one tower to the other. The road or pathway hangs from these cables, creating a dramatic appearance.
4. Cable-stayed Bridge: Look for bridges with towers and cables running directly from the towers to the road or pathway, forming a fan-like pattern. The cables support the road from above, giving a unique and modern look.
5. Truss Bridge: Search for images of bridges with a framework of beams forming triangles, known as trusses. They often have a crisscross pattern on the sides and can vary in design.
6. Tied Arch Bridge: Find images of bridges with arches that are tied together at the top with horizontal beams. They typically have a bow-like appearance and are quite striking.

Skyscraper

A skyscraper is like a giant tower that reaches way up into the sky!

Imagine stacking up a bunch of toy blocks really high – that's kind of what a skyscraper is like, but on a much bigger scale! Skyscrapers are super cool because they're so tall that they can fit lots of offices, apartments, or shops inside. They're like their own little city in one big building!

People build skyscrapers in busy cities where there isn't a lot of space left on the ground. Instead of spreading outwards, they build upwards into the sky!

Some famous skyscrapers you might have heard of are the Empire State Building in New York City, the Burj Khalifa in Dubai, and the Shanghai Tower in China. They're all really tall and look amazing against the skyline!

So, next time you look up and see a super tall building reaching into the clouds, you'll know it's a skyscraper – a towering symbol of human ingenuity and engineering!

Famous Skyscrapers

V X U S J I N M A O T O W E R N C I O F M S Z O
T H B H A Y E K G N I K T G A E L R O C A K M Q
M F M M Q K C W Z V J G R L O T T E D N E O R A
Z A T I R E T N E C N A H U W N V X O Z F N A V
O N T U U N F Z D A E D Q I M T X R U U U E S O
Q I D U G B F R U H V X U M A L T D O G S W Y I
L R Z S K Q I G W R D I D I P E U H X M J O E M
O A M K E G N K G N G E P J P A Z G I S S R R I
D M G N X W A V V J A E Y I T G O Z Z W T L G C
W G E N G C N O N Z I G I O N R R M X F J D Y C
Q U E O H C C T Q B P P N A L K A C M X T T I B
S T G B U Z E Q U Q R X U I M J M Z U X O R S U
E M H L J F D B G P C G Z Y P D T U U R I A U R
U F N B X U O R W N M O C F Z C H D N Z I D G J
W V A B R A J A L B A I T C L O C K T O W E R K
N P R E W O T S I L L I W Z Z Y Y Y X K C C C H
S F T X H D I A H G N A H S B T T I D J E E S A
Y K N F E O A A D S Q D N B A K G O D B O N U L
A A D U I R E W O T G N E F I Z U T E S Q T K I
Q W G N I D L I U B E T A T S E R I P M E E N F
P A R K A V E N U E N T O N V F P L M G H R G A
T R U M P T O W E R W G W S Y K P F A I O G Z F
X D J C Z N N C C Y X V B F T S U F L A P L L Z
N Q D D C Y O U K K Z P L T W O Y D W V J Y H Q

Abraj Al-Bait Clock Tower
Jin Mao Tower
Willis Tower
Shanghai
Park Avenue

Domes

A dome is a big, round roof that covers a building. It's like a giant, upside-down bowl! Imagine a giant bubble on top of a building – that's kind of what a dome looks like!

Now, here's the cool part: because of its shape, a dome can hold itself up without needing any support in the middle. That means it can cover a big space inside without anything blocking it!

Engineers use math and science to design domes that are strong enough to stay up, even when it's windy or there's a lot of weight on top.

Saint paul's cathedral

Saint Basil's cathedral

The Blue Mosque

Domes are used in lots of buildings, like churches, stadiums, and even some houses! So, when you see a big, round roof on a building, you'll know it's a dome and that engineers worked hard to make it strong and beautiful!

A Dome for a Loving Wife

Colour The Taj Mahal

Digging a Canal

Imagine you have a big bathtub with a divider in the middle. On one side of the divider, you pour water from a jug, and it starts to fill up that side of the tub. Once it's full, you open a little door in the divider, and the water flows through to the other side. That's kind of how a canal works!

The Panama Canal is a very big canal, but it works on the same idea. Ships sail into the canal from one side, and then they go through a series of locks. These locks are like giant water elevators. They lift the ship up to a higher level, and then the ship can continue sailing through the canal. Once the ship reaches the other side, it goes through another set of locks to lower it back down to sea level.

It's like a shortcut for ships, and it helps them travel faster and save time and money!

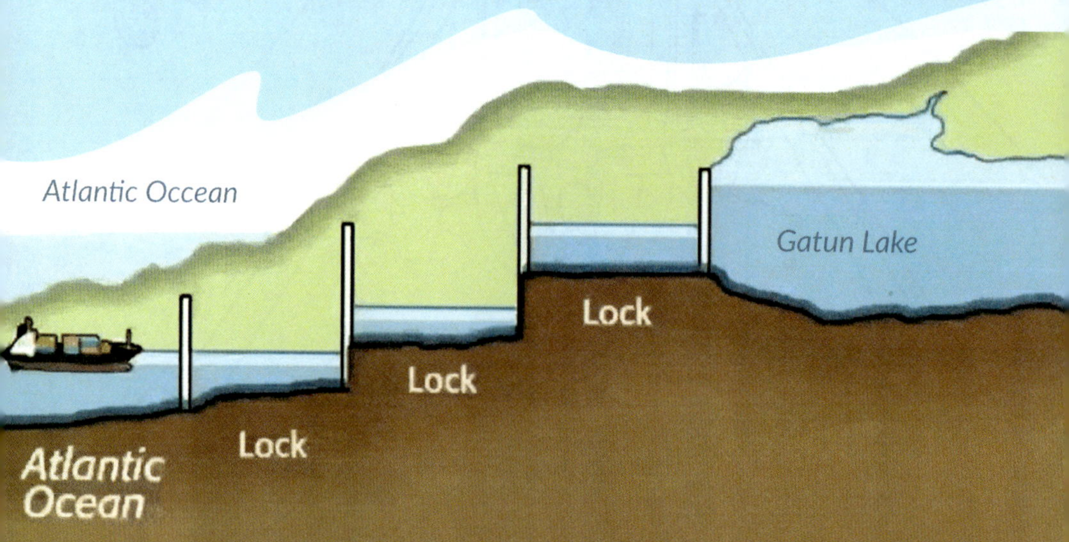

Observe the map and answer

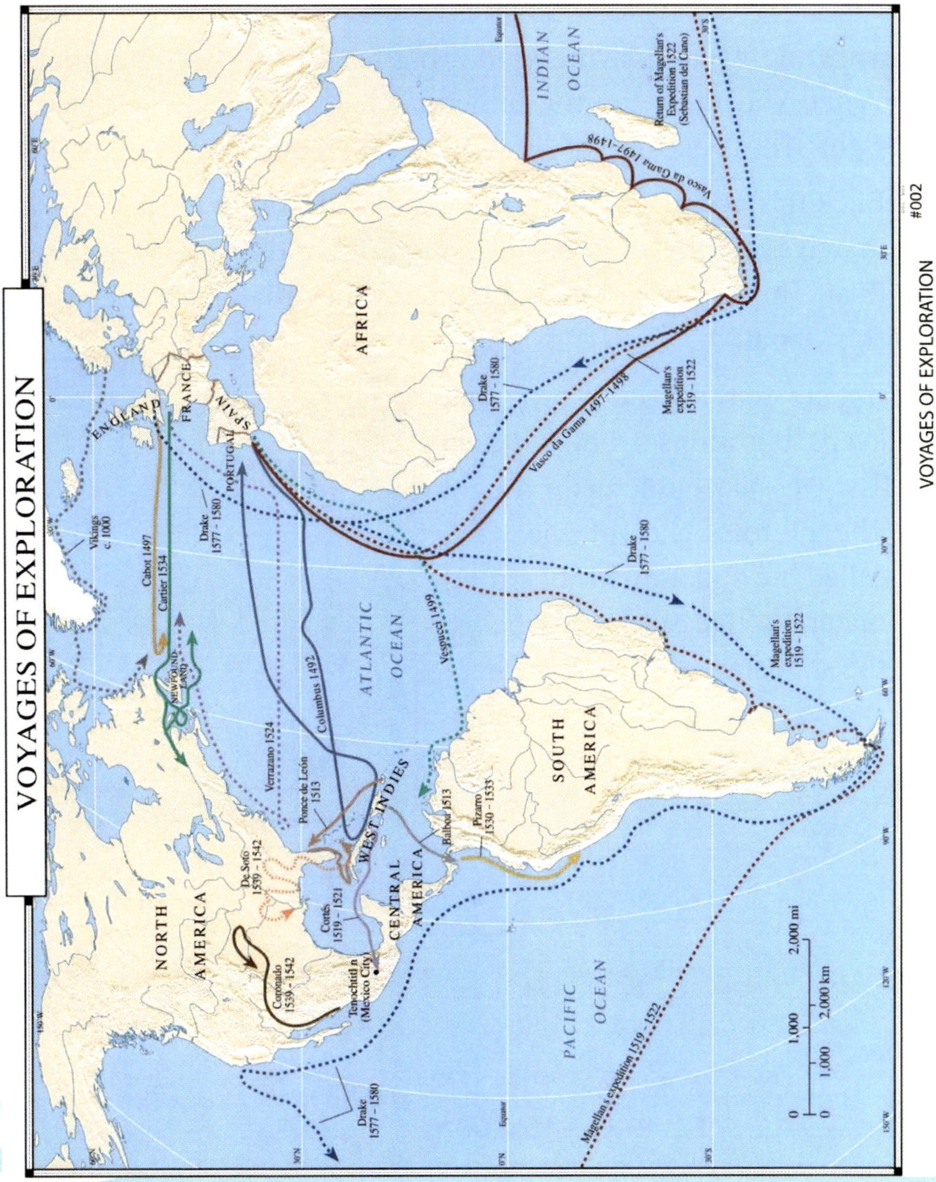

(a) How long did it take Magellan to circle the globe?

Ans. ....

(b) When Ferdinand Magellan left Spain in 1519, which direction did he set sail?

Ans. ....

Why don't big ships sink?

Imagine you're playing with a big toy in a swimming pool. When you push the toy underwater, it pops right back up, right? That's because of something called buoyancy.

Big ships are like gigantic versions of those toys. They're so massive that they push a lot of water out of the way when they float. This creates a force called buoyancy that helps keep the ship afloat.

But it's not just buoyancy that keeps big ships from sinking. They're also built really tough! The bottom part of the ship, called the hull, is made of strong materials like steel. This helps the ship stay sturdy even when it's sailing through rough waters.

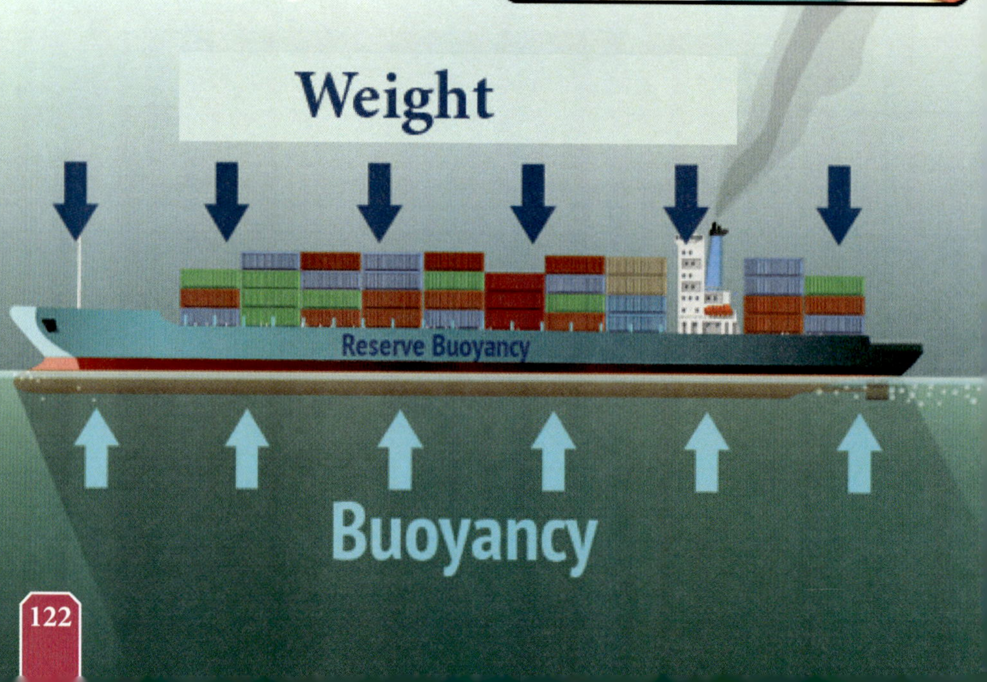

Spot 10 differences

Answer the following questions :-

(a) Name a very fast sailing ship of 19th century.

Ans. ....

(b) Name the ship which moves underwater.

Ans. ....

(c) Kitchen of a ship is called as?

Ans. ....

(c) Top of the boat is called as?

Ans. ....

How does a submarine work?

A submarine (or any boat) can float when the mass of water that it displaces (pushes out of the way) is equal to the mass of the boat. This displaced water causes an upward force called buoyancy. Buoyancy acts in the opposite direction to gravity, which would pull the ship down. A regular boat cannot control or change its buoyancy, but a submarine can. This allows a submarine to dive under the water or to come up to the surface. To control its buoyancy, the submarine has ballast tanks that can be filled with water or filled with air. When the submarine is on the surface, the ballast tanks are filled with air. This makes the submarine's density less than the density of the water. When the submarine dives, water is pumped into the ballast tanks to replace the air.

S.O.S.
S.O.S.
S.O.S.

How does an Airplane Fly ?

Imagine you're outside on a windy day, and you have a kite. When you hold up the kite and the wind catches it, it starts to fly up into the sky, right? Well, airplanes work kind of like that! The science of flight is called aerodynamics. Four main aerodynamic forces act on an airplane in flight. They are called drag, thrust, gravity (or weight), and lift.

As a plane flies, the air slows it down. This is the effect of drag. To overcome drag, a plane needs the forward-moving force of thrust. Thrust is produced by the plane's engines or propellers.

An airplane is heavier than air. It will fall to the ground under the influence of gravity unless lift is applied. The plane's wings are able to produce the necessary lift because of their shape. The upper surface is curved, while the lower surface is flat. To

get past the curved surface, the air that flows over the wing has to go farther—and therefore faster—than the air that flows under it. This creates a difference in air pressure between the upper and lower surfaces as the plane moves forward. The air underneath is under greater pressure and therefore pushes the wing up. The faster the air flows past the wings, the greater the lift. For this reason, an airplane takes off most easily when it faces the wind.

Pilots use flaps and slats to change the amount of lift. Lowering the flaps increases the curved surface of the wing, which provides more lift for takeoff. Slats also increase lift by allowing air to flow more smoothly over the wing. Raising the flaps reduces lift, which slows down the plane for landing.

Colour the picture

Sooo cooooooold !

Most people would not know what to do without a refrigerator, as there are few things that can soothe their dried-out throat as much as a glass of chilled water.

Refrigerators are amazing machines. The principle of refrigeration and cooling is very simple: it involves removing heat from one region and depositing it in another.

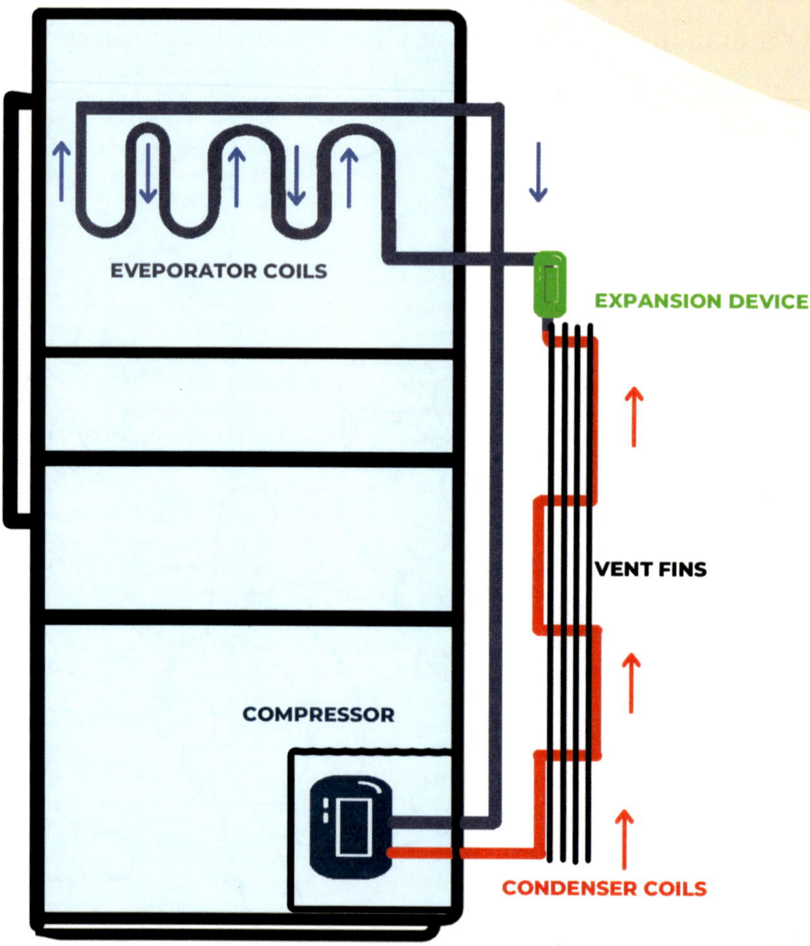

When you pass a low-temperature liquid close to objects that you want to cool, heat from those objects is transferred to the liquid, which evaporates (and converts to gas) and takes away the heat in the process. This process involves a mechanism with refrigerant gas, heat exchanger coils, and a compressor.

You may already know that gases heat up when you compress them and cool down when they are allowed to expand. That's why a bicycle pump feels warm when you use it to pump air into a tire, while sprayed perfume feels cold.

SPOT THE DIFFERENCES!

What's a Thermostat ?

Imagine you have a special friend who helps keep your room just the right temperature, neither too hot nor too cold. That friend is called a thermostat!

A thermostat has a little sensor inside that can feel how warm or cold it is in the room. It's like a tiny superhero that knows when things need to change.

If the room gets too warm, the thermostat knows it's time to cool things down. It sends a signal to the air conditioner to start blowing cool air. On the other hand, if it's too cold, the thermostat tells the heater to turn on and warm things up. The thermostat's job is to keep everything balanced, like a seesaw. So, a thermostat is like a smart friend that helps control the temperature in your room. It keeps things not too hot, not too cold, but just right for you to feel super comfortable!

Colour the cold and hot objects

Hot things in red tones

Cold things in Blue tones

What is Thermometer

A more accurate way to measure temperature is by using a thermometer. A thermometer is the instrument used to tell the air temperature. A thermometer is usually made up of a small, hollow glass tube. At the bottom of the tube is a bulb, which holds a liquid such as alcohol or mercury.

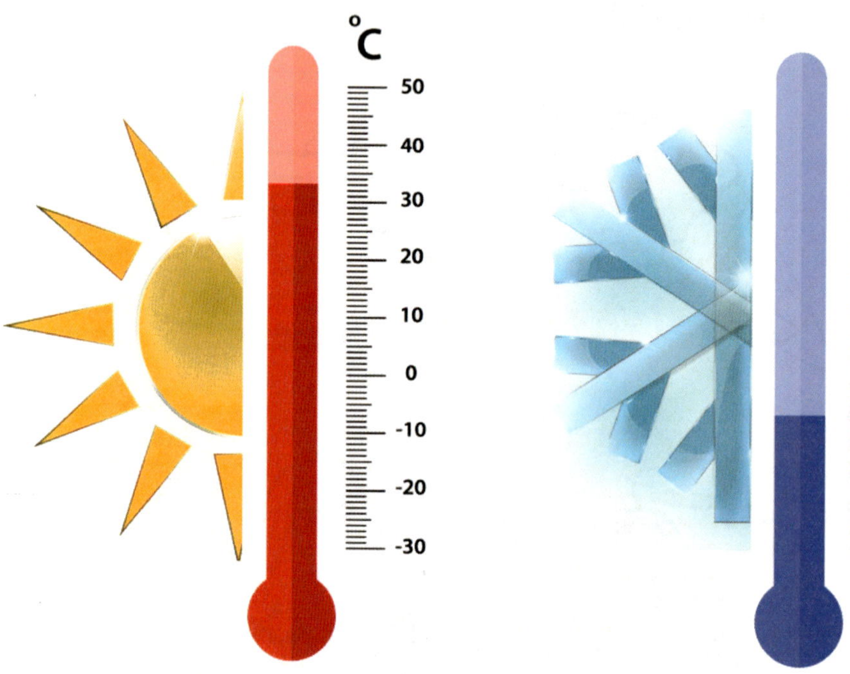

When there is an increase in heat, the liquid inside the bulb expands, pushing up into the tube. A decrease in heat lets the liquid contract, moving down the tube. A measuring scale is attached to the tube, to give an accurate measurement of heat energy.

Temprature

(a) What do you wear when it's really hot outside?

Ans. : ....

(b) What's your favorite thing to do when it's cold?

Ans. : ....

(c) How does your body feel when you're playing in the snow?

Ans. : ....

Engine

An engine, or motor, is a machine used to change energy into movement that can be used. The energy can be in any form. Common forms of energy used in engines are electricity, chemical (such as petrol or diesel) or heat. When a chemical is used to produce energy it is known as fuel.

The difference of engine and motor is that an engine creates mechanical energy from heat, while motor creates mechanical energy from other kinds of energy, like electricity. Typical engines are steam engine and internal combustion or piston engine, while typical motors are electric motor and hydraulic motor.

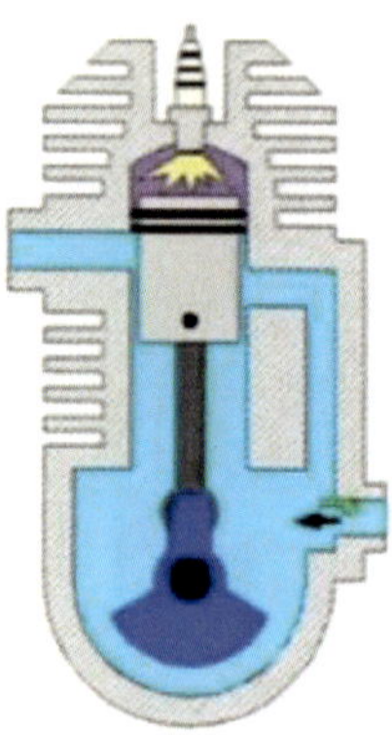

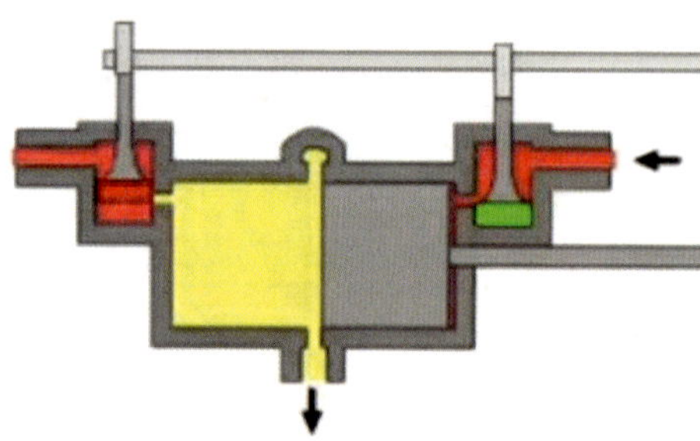

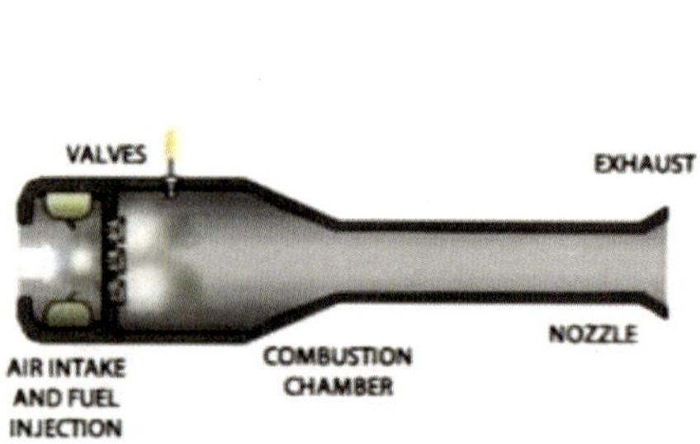

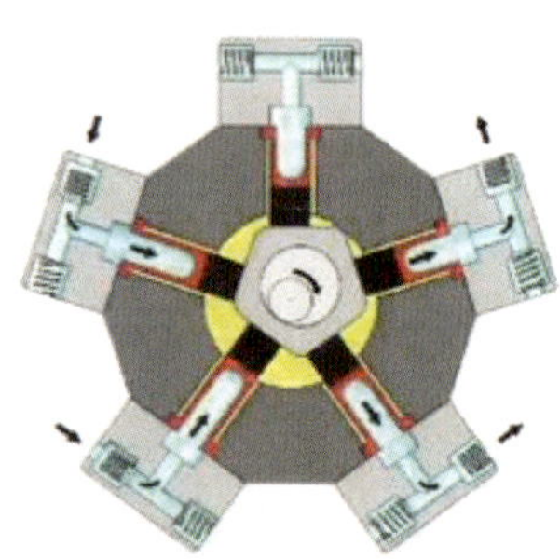

Piston Engine

Most of the cars on the road today need to fuel up with gasoline. Why do cars and trucks need gasoline to run? Car engines are often called internal combustion engines. A car engine ignites a mixture of air and gasoline. The force of that explosion causes the engine's pistons to move up and down. In turn, the pistons turn a crankshaft. That crankshaft turns the tyres on the car. The rotation of the tyres allows a vehicle to travel down the road.

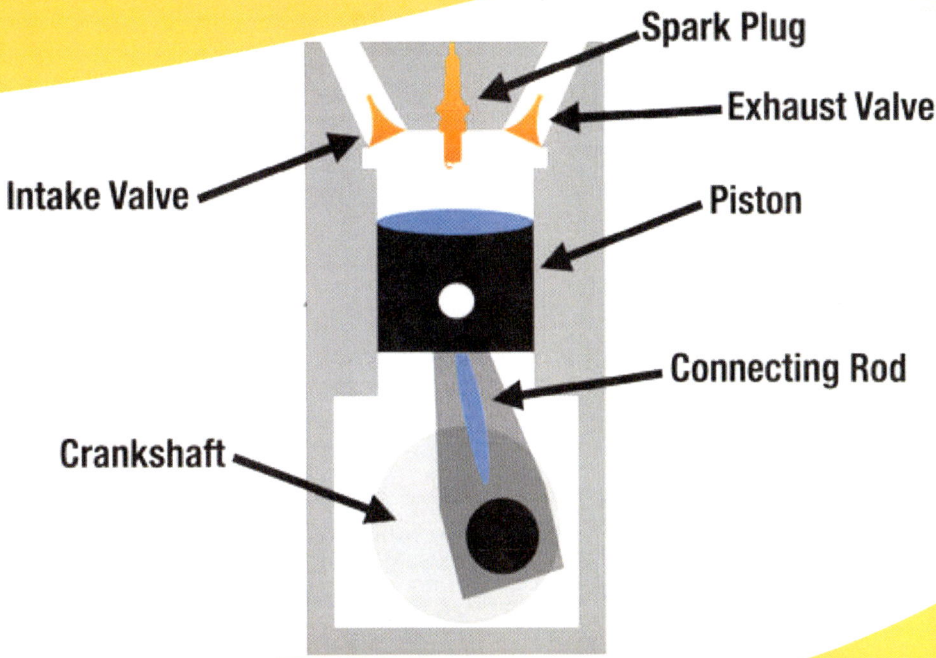

Jet Engine

A jet engine is a type of air-breathing turbine engine, often used on aircraft. The principle of all jet engines is essentially the same. The engine draws air in at the front and compresses it. The air then combines with fuel and the engine burns the resulting mixture. The combustion greatly increases the volume of the gases which are then exhausted out of the rear of the engine.

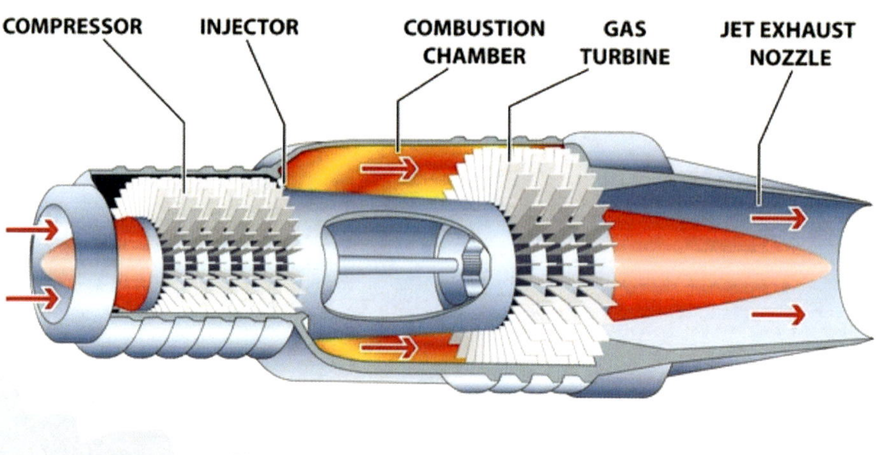

Nuclear Engine

Nuclear power plants heat water to produce steam. The steam is used to spin large turbines that generate electricity. Nuclear power plants use heat produced during nuclear fission to heat water.

In nuclear fission, atoms are split apart to form smaller atoms, releasing energy. Fission takes place inside the reactor of a nuclear power plant. At the center of the reactor is the core, which contains uranium fuel.

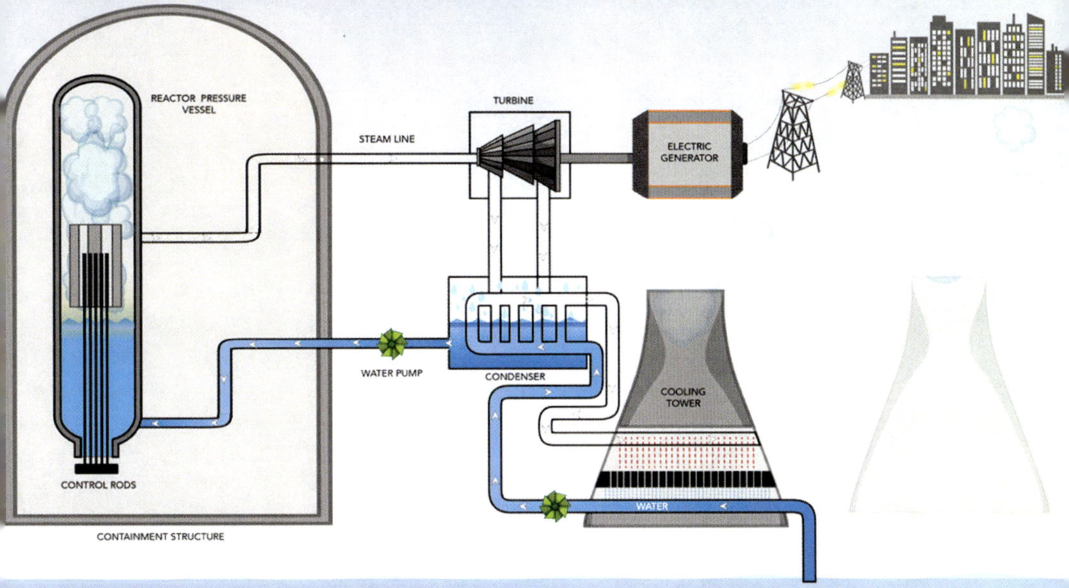

Telescope

A telescope is an instrument that allows people to see distant objects. Telescopes are important tools in astronomy. Telescopes have helped scientists discover new planets, stars, galaxies, and other objects in space. They've also helped us learn more about our own solar system and the universe. So, in simple terms, a telescope is like a magical window that helps us explore the wonders of space! There are several different types

of telescopes. Some, called light telescopes, gather light from objects. Other telescopes gather different kinds of information about the object being viewed.

Colour the Picture

Microscope

Microscope is a really cool tool that helps us see things that are too small to see with our naked eyes. It's like a super magnifying glass! Microscopes are used in all kinds of fields, from science and medicine to research and education. They've

helped scientists discover tiny organisms, study cells and tissues, and even explore the structure of molecules!

Find the objects

Find 15 objects in the picture

It's Electric

Electricity flows in a circuit from the negative pole of a battery to its positive pole. The flow of electricity creates an electric current. Many things need electricity to work. Batteries are one source of electricity. Electricity can also be obtained by plugging things into a socket in the wall. This electricity comes from wires that go into your home.

Find which machine is ON

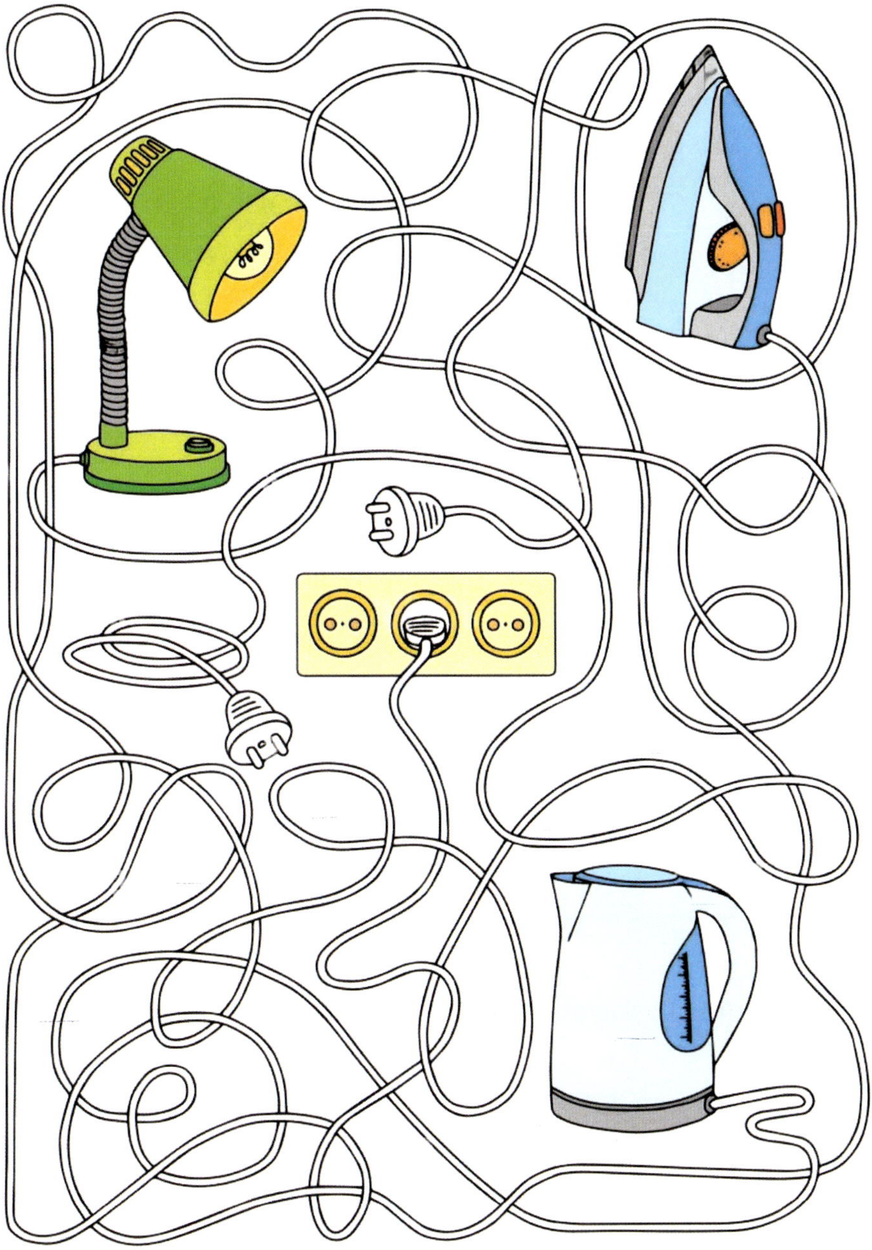

STEAM

ARTS

Juice-Pouch Stomp Rocket

This rocket from Ana Dziengel of Babble Dabble Doo uses the power of compressed air to launch into the sky. (Budding engineers take note: This is called pneumatics!)

What You'll Need:

1. Empty juice pouch
2. One flexible straw (that comes with the pouch)
3. One standard straw
4. Colored cardstock
5. Washi tape (optional)
6. Modeling clay and scissor

What To Do:

1. Snip off the end of the flexible straw on an angle.
2. Insert the pointed end of the straw into the straw hole of the juice pouch.
3. Cut the second straw in half. This will be your rocket.
4. Make three trapezoids from cardstock, in the following dimensions: 3 inches (base) x 1 inch (height) x 3/4 inches (top). Set two aside to be full fins. Cut the last one in half vertically.
5. Tape the full fins on each side of the straw. Don't flatten the straw.
6. Tape one half-fin perpendicularly to each full fin as shown. Add washi tape to decorate the straw if desired.
7. Roll a small bit of clay into a ball. Add this to the top to seal the straw completely.
8. To launch the rocket, inflate the pouch by blowing into the flexible straw. Bend the flexible straw to aim and place the rocket straw over the end. Stomp down hard for liftoff!

Note: If after some use, one of the straws cracks, simply replace it with a new one.

Pom-Pom Catapult

This simple machine uses stored energy (the tension in the rubber bands) to release a projectile (called the payload).

What You'll Need:

1. Hole punch
2. Rectangular box
3. Three unsharpened pencils
4. A few strong rubber bands
5. Masking tape or glue
6. Jar lid and paper clip

What To Do:

1. Punch a hole in a long side of the box, 3 inches from a short side.
2. Punch a matching hole on the other side. The holes should be large to rotate a pencil easily. Punch a third hole on the opposite side; it should be centered and near the bottom.
3. Assemble the catapult arm: Join 2 pencils together perpendicularly to make an inverted lowercase t; secure them with rubber bands.
4. Tape or glue a small jar lid to the longer end of the arm
5. Wrap another rubber band around the shorter end of the arm using a slipknot.
6. Place the ends of the horizontal pencil in the side holes.
7. Thread the tail of the slipknot (from Step 4) through the remaining hole, and knot a paper clip around the end to hold it in place.
8. Create a "stopper" for the catapult arm with the third pencil. Place it across the top of the box just in front of the arm; secure it in place by wrapping a large rubber band around one end of the pencil, under the box, and up and around the other end. Load it up, and let 'er fly.

Electric Play-Doh Lightning Bug

In this STEAM activity, kids will create a simple closed circuit to make their bug glow.

What You'll Need:

1. Cardstock
2. Play-Doh
3. 10mm diffused LED bulb with leads
4. Four AA batteries
5. Four AA battery pack with leads
6. Scissors

What To Do:

1. Cut an oval cardstock base for the bug and two heart-shaped wings.
2. From Play-Doh, make the head and two separate, oblong sides; place them on the paper base. (Make sure the side pieces don't touch each other or the bug won't light up.)
3. Add eyes and antennae as you like.
4. Look at the leads of the LED. The longer one is the positive lead, and the shorter one is the negative.
5. Pull the leads apart, and stick one end into each side of the body. Remember which side has the positive lead.
6. Insert the batteries into the battery pack. Stick the red wire into the side with the positive LED lead; put the black wire into the other.
7. Turn on the battery pack and watch the bug glow!

Note: If your bug doesn't light up, turn the LED around and insert the long lead into the other side of the body.

Balance Sculpture

Your budding builders will need to be patient as they test to find the sweet spot to make it balance!

What You'll Need:

1. Cardboard
2. Craft paint
3. Paper-towel tube
4. 5-inch square piece of cardboard
5. Hot glue
6. Scissors
7. Floral wire or pipe cleaners
8. Beads
9. 12-inch bamboo skewer with sharp ends snipped off

What To Do:

1. Cut the cardboard into shapes; paint. Paint the paper-towel tube and square piece of cardboard. Let dry.
2. Flatten one end of the paper-towel tube; staple closed. Cut a small V-shaped notch in the center of the flattened end. This will be the fulcrum.
3. Glue the open end of the paper-towel tube to the cardboard square (adult supervision needed). Let dry.
4. Thread cardboard shapes, wire, and beads onto a long skewer, balancing and adjusting it on the notch.
5. Continue adjusting, using tape if needed for security, until the sculpture is balanced.

Invisible Ink

When life gives you lemons, make a secret message from invisible ink!

What You'll Need:

1. One lemon
2. Cotton swab
3. Sheet of white paper
4. Sunlight, iron, or lightbulb

What To Do:

1. Squeeze the lemon juice into a bowl and add a spoonful of water.
2. Mix gently. Dip the swab into the liquid and write a message or draw a picture on the paper.
3. Let the liquid dry completely so that the message or picture is invisible. To share your secret, set it in sunlight, hold it close to a lightbulb, or iron (with adult help).
4. The message will be revealed! Hang it as artwork, or share it with a friend.

How Does It Work?

Diluting or adding water to the lemon juice makes it very hard to see when you apply it to the paper, but lemon juice is an organic substance that oxidizes and turns brown when it's heated up. This means that no one will notice that the secret is there until the paper is heated and the message is revealed! Other substances that work in the same way include orange juice, honey diluted with water, milk, onion juice, and vinegar.

Solar System

This far-out felting project is to get the kids psyched to go back to science class.

What You'll Need:

1. About 2 oz of 100% wool roving in assorted colors
2. Two 38-gauge star-point felting needles (adult supervision needed)
3. Felting pad or dense foam
4. White fiberfill stuffing
5. White paint and Two paint-stirring sticks
6. Drill and 3/32-inch drill bit (adult supervision needed)
7. White baker's twine or thin cotton yarn
8. Sewing needle with a large eye
9. Brass fish-eye hook
10. Small brass chain

Solar System

What To Do:

1. To make a planet, pull off a few inches of roving and roll it into a ball so it fits in your palm.
2. Pin onto the felt pad with one needle and use the other to "felt," or to press the needle up and down repeatedly. The tiny barbs on the end of the felting needle compress the fibers into a desired shape.
3. Turn the roving often and continue felting until it forms a semi-firm and uniform ball. Felt on a thin piece of roving in a different color if desired (to make the blue swirls on Neptune, for instance). Repeat to make additional planets.
4. To make the sun, pull a 4- to 5-inch-diameter tuft of stuffing and wrap it with yellow roving to cover stuffing completely.
5. Paint two paint-stirring sticks and let dry. Mark five holes, spaced about 3 inches apart, on one of the paint sticks. Drill. Place the drilled stick over the other one as a template, mark holes, and drill.
6. With the sticks in an "X" shape, line up the center holes; use the needle to thread the sun through the center hole. Knot to desired length.
7. Twist in the fish-eye hook from the top to secure the paint sticks together. Secure the planets to yarn with the needle and thread up through remaining eight holes.
8. Knot in place at desired heights. Add a chain to hang; felt on small amounts of wool to planets as needed to balance the mobile.

Bath Bombs

Scrub-a-dub-dub! Add some science to the tub with these pretty and so-simple bath bombs from Curious Jane.

What You'll Need:

1. 1/2 cup citric acid, 1 cup baking soda
2. 1/2 cup cornstarch, 1/2 cup Epsom salt
3. Essential oil of your choice,1 tsp water, 1 tsp olive oil
4. Sphere-shaped mold (we used clear plastic ornaments)

What To Do:

1. Combine citric acid, baking soda, cornstarch, and Epsom salt in a large bowl. Mix well and set aside. In a small bowl, mix together one or two drops of essential oil, water, and olive oil.
2. Add the wet mixture to the dry very slowly. Mix it together quickly and thoroughly so it doesn't begin to bubble.
3. Once it's all combined, let the mixture sit for a few minutes; it should look and feel like wet sand. If it's still too dry, add a drop of olive oil, but don't oversaturate.
4. Separate the mixture into smaller bowls and add food coloring, mixing in the color by hand.
5. Layer the different colors in both halves of a sphere-shaped mold and pack them down. When each side is completely filled with a slight mound, press them together and gently rotate until the sides lock.
6. Let the bomb dry in the mold for a few minutes, then carefully remove the top half. Leave it for another hour or two, then carefully turn the bottom half out of the mold.
7. Let it dry overnight.

Dancing Puppet

Surprise: The whole robot moves with the pull of a string!

What You'll Need:

1. Paint and paintbrush
2. A piece of cardboard cut into 13 strips that are 1½-inch-wide (four 10-inch pieces, four 5-inch pieces, one 4-inch piece, and four 3½-inch pieces)
3. Construction paper
4. Pencil
5. Scissors
6. Hole punch
7. 1-inch-capacity brads
8. Glue
9. 6-inch piece of string

What To Do:

1. Paint one side of each cardboard piece black; let dry. Trace the robot-face template onto construction paper and cut out; fold as directed.
2. Following the template, punch holes in the cardboard pieces and connect the face and cardboard pieces with brads.
3. Score the 4-inch piece of cardboard into sections, then fold it into a T and glue it to the back of the puppet; let dry.
4. Tie the string to the bottom-most brad.
5. Hold the puppet by the handle and pull on the string to get the arms and legs moving.

Pentominoes

Pentominoes are shapes made from groups of congruent squares.

What You'll Need:

1. Glue
2. 60 unfinished 1-inch wooden cubes (we got ours on amazon.com)
3. Paintbrush
4. Paint in color(s) of your choice

What To Do:

1. Sort the wooden cubes into groups of five, then challenge your child to create 12 different shapes where each cube .
2. Share atleast one side with another. These are your pentominoes! (Use the photo as a key if they get stuck.)
3. Once your child has found all 12 configurations, glue the cubes together and paint them as desired. (We mixed teal with increasing amounts of white paint for an ombré set.)
4. Time to play! Have your child try to create various squares and rectangles with the blocks. (Hint: They'll need four different puzzle pieces to complete a 4 x 5 rectangle.)

Math Fact Triangles

Most parents learned to solve problems in a linear way: 1 + 2 = 3. Using the triangles helps kids think in "fact families." They learn that 1 + 2 = 3 and 3 - 2 = 1 at the same time.

What You'll Need:

1. Craft foam in various colors
2. Scissors
3. Sharpie pen

What To Do:

1. Cut out equal-sized triangles from different colors of craft foam.
2. Along with your child, use a Sharpie to write an addition/subtraction or multiplication/division equation (depending on your child's skills) on each triangle, placing one number in each corner; circle the answer.
3. Flip the triangles over. Choose one, cover the circled answer with your finger, and ask your child to solve it. (To practice the opposite operation, cover one of the other numbers.)

Perler Bead Arrays

Take a break from flash cards and practice multiplication tables using arrays, which allow kids to see the answers as they study.

What You'll Need:

1. Perler beads (we got ours from Amazon)
2. Perler beads clear square pegboards (such as this set)
3. Iron

What To Do:

1. Write out an equation (say, 7 x 3), then challenge your child to express it with Perler beads as an array of three columns of seven.
2. Then count the total number of beads to figure out the answer.
3. If your child is struggling with particular equations or a line on their multiplication tables, create a permanent version for them to use: For each equation (7 x 1, 7 x 2, etc), have your child help you assemble the correct number of beads into an array (so one column of seven, two columns of seven, etc.), then (with your assistance) iron to set according to package directions.
4. Break them out whenever they need some practice.

DIY Scratch Paper

This STEAM activity for kids involves making your own color-scratch cards and sending a magical message.

What You'll Need:

1. Blank white cards
2. Crayons
3. Masking tape
4. 2 tbsp clear detergent
5. 2 tbsp black acrylic paint
6. Paintbrush
7. Small plastic mixing bowl
8. Spoon

What To Do:

1. Tape down the card with masking tape around the edges.
2. Color in completely with a rainbow of crayons.
3. Mix the black acrylic paint and clear detergent in a small bowl.
4. Paint the card with the mixture, and allow it to dry. Do at least two coats.
5. When completely dry, slowly and carefully peel the masking tape away. Scratch your message into the card with a
6. Coin or the pointed end of the paintbrush, and see the colors revealed!

DIY Ice-Cream

In this STEAM activity for kids, you'll make ice cream by surrounding the ingredients with a layer of even colder ice.

What You'll Need:

1. One quart-sized zip-top bag
2. One gallon-sized zip-top bag
3. 4 cups ice
4. 6 tbsp rock salt
5. 1/2 cup half-and-half
6. 1 tbsp vanilla extract
7. 1 tbsp white sugar

What To Do:

1. Add the ice and rock salt to the gallon-sized bag. Shake to coat.
2. Combine half-and-half, sugar, extract, and a pinch of salt in the quart-sized bag. Seal it tight, getting all the air out.
3. Nestle the small bag of ice cream mixture into the large bag of ice, so that the ice surrounds it. Seal the large bag tightly.
4. Now shake, shake, shake it up! After about 5 minutes, your sweet treat will be ready to eat!

Sand Pendulum

This STEAM activity for kids creates a pendulum—esse-tially a weight that hangs freely from a string

What You'll Need:

1. Yarn
2. Scissors
3. Sturdy rubber band
4. Kitchen funnel
5. Broomstick or dowel
6. Poster paper (to catch the sand)
7. Craft sand

What To Do:

1. Cut three lengths of yarn, each about 3 inches long. Tie each piece to the rubber band, spacing them equally apart Slip the rubber band over the funnel so that it fits tightly under the lip.
2. Gather the strings above the funnel and tie them at the top so that the funnel hangs evenly.
3. Suspend the funnel from a broomstick or dowel (or just hold it). Place paper below to catch the sand.
4. Have your child fill the funnel with sand, blocking the small opening of the funnel with their finger as they fill it.

Instruct them to remove their finger and give it a little push.

STEAM

MATHS

What Are Numbers?

A number is basically a way to count or measure things. It's like when you count how many candies you have or how tall someone is. Numbers can be big or small, like 1, 2, 3, and so on. Basically, whenever you need to say "how many" or "how much," you're using numbers!

Some 2,000 years ago, the ancient Roman created a system of numbers. We call them roman numerals. Instead of using digits like we do with 1, 2, 3, they used letters. You can find Roman numerals on the faces of some clocks.

I = 1

V = 5

X = 10

L = 50

C = 100

D = 500

M = 1,000

Roman Numeral Sudoku

Sudoku is like a puzzle game that you play on a grid. The grid is divided into smaller squares, and some of these squares already have numbers in them. Your job is to fill in the empty squares with numbers from 1 to 9.

This puzzle has a twist. It contains Roman numerals. See if you can solve it.

This puzzle has a twist. It contains Roman numerals. See if you can solve it.

V				IV	III
IV		I	II		VI
		III		I	
II				VI	
			IV	II	
I	II	IV	VI		V

Even and Odd Numbers

There are two types of numbers. Some of even numbers and others are odd numbers. Even numbers are like pairs of socks. You can divide them evenly between two people, with no socks left over. Examples are 2, 4, 6, 8, and so on.

Odd numbers are like groups of three friends. If you try to share something equally between them, there's always one friend who doesn't get a share. Examples are 1, 3, 5, 7, and so on.

	5		3	1	4		6	
8	7				9	4		3
6	4	3	5		7	1	9	2
		7	8		5	2	1	
4	1		9					
	2	5		6	1	9		7
7	9		2	5		8	4	
		4		5	6			5
	3		1		8	6	7	

Count the Star

Count the star and write how many of each there are. Then decide whether the numbers are odd or even

(a) 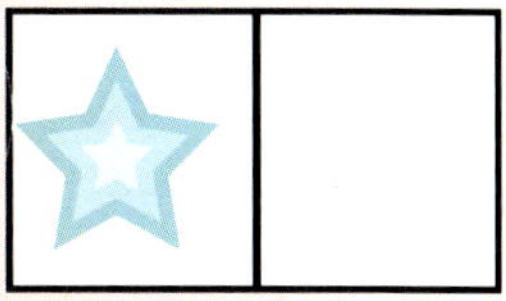

(b) 

(c) 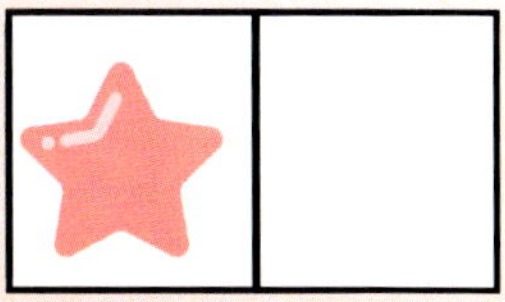

Comparing Quantities

Comparing quantities means figuring out which one is more, less, or if they are the same.

For example, let's say you have a basket of apples and a basket of oranges. If you count the apples and there are 5, and then count the oranges and there are 3, you can say that there are more apples than oranges.

But sometimes, you might have the same number of things in each group. For instance, if you have 2 toy cars and 2 toy trucks, then you have the same amount in each group.

Comparing quantities is like figuring out who has more cookies or if you have the same number of candies as your friend. It's a way to understand which group has more, less, or if they're equal.

Put the sign (=, >, <)

At All Adds Up

If want to find out how many you have of something, you need to add them up. Adding things is simple. It doesn't matter which way the numbers appear; the total, or sum, is always the same. For example, 4+6=10 as does 6+4. You can even add more than one number.

+11		+10		+6
	+6			
+9			**2**	**1**
+5			+9	
	+13			**3**

+9		+9		+5
	+7			
+10			**2**	**3**
1	+5		4	5
+8			+7	**2**

Add the Boxes

The goal of each puzzle is to fill in the grid with numbers.

The only numbers you may write are 1,2,3,4,5.

No number amy appear more than once in any row or cuolumn.

When you see a heavy borders, that means there's a target numbers. That number is in the left-hand corner of one box. All the numbers within the heavy border must add up to the target number.

Numbers may be repeated in the border area as long as they do not repeat within a single row or coloumn.

Some boxes have been filled in with numbers.

+8		+7		+6
	+11		5	
2		+6		
+8		+7		
+5		2	+8	

A-Mazing Numbers

Help the honeybees get to the flowers. Make a path by drawing a line through the boxes that have a sum of 8, 10 or 12

		10 + 2 = 12	6 + 4	11 + 1	10 + 5
12 + 2	4 + 3	11 + 7	1 + 2	4 + 4	7 + 2
13 + 1	4 + 8	2 + 10	9 + 1	7 + 1	14 + 3
6 + 2	3 + 7	7 + 4	9 + 4	3 + 3	13 + 3
8 + 2	4 + 11	3 + 5	1 + 7	8 + 2	15 + 1
5 + 7	5 + 5	9 + 3	9 + 9		

Help the fish get out of the maze. Make a path by drawing a line through the boxes that have a sum of 7, 11, or 17.

10 + 1	14 + 3	3 + 8	10 + 8	14 + 5	
1 + 6	12 + 2			9 + 3	16 + 1
5 + 2	6 + 11	12 + 4	3 + 3	6 + 1	15 + 2
11 + 1	2 + 15	2 + 9	3 + 16	4 + 3	7 + 7
12 + 1	1 + 8	6 + 5	1 + 5	3 + 14	8 + 7
14 + 2	5 + 9	6 + 1	9 + 8	4 + 7	10 + 8

All Set?

A set is like a special group of things that belong together. Imagine you have a collection of toys – all the red cars could be in one set, and all the blue trucks could be in another set.

Set is a collection of numbers or objects. Each item in the set is called an element. For example, a set of fruits might include apples, oranges, and bananas. Each fruit is an element of the set.

Sets can also be used in fun activities, like sorting different types of toys or organizing your favorite snacks. They help us group things together based on their similarities. So, next time you're organizing your toys or snacks, think of sets as your helpful tool!

Set and More Sets

Wrtite the missing numbers in the empty shapes

2 sets of ___ = 8

2 sets of 3 = ___

3 sets of ___ = ___

Summing It up

15 + 35	57
17 + 40	68
22 + 33	95
36 + 28	88
10 + 12	56
43 + 52	64
34 + 54	22
18 + 38	55
32 + 35	39
24 + 15	67
18 + 50	30
12 + 18	50

Addition

Addition isone of the four basic operations of arithmetic. It is bringing two or more numbers (or things) together to make a new total.

The Additon Table

+	0	1	2	3	4	5	6	7	8	9	10	11	12
0	0	1	2	3	4	5	6	7	8	9	10	11	12
1	1	2	3	4	5	6	7	8	9	10	11	12	13
2	2	3	4	5	6	7	8	9	10	11	12	13	14
3	3	4	5	6	7	8	9	10	11	12	13	14	15
4	4	5	6	7	8	9	10	11	12	13	14	15	16
5	5	6	7	8	9	10	11	12	13	14	15	16	17
6	6	7	8	9	10	11	12	13	14	15	16	17	18
7	7	8	9	10	11	12	13	14	15	16	17	18	19
8	8	9	10	11	12	13	14	15	16	17	18	19	20
9	9	10	11	12	13	14	15	16	17	18	19	20	21
10	10	11	12	13	14	15	16	17	18	19	20	21	22
11	11	12	13	14	15	16	17	18	19	20	21	22	23
12	12	13	14	15	16	17	18	19	20	21	22	23	24

The Addition Table

The addition table can help you as you learn to add

1		3		
	7		9	
			13	
		15		
			19	

Fill in the missing number on each addition wheel.

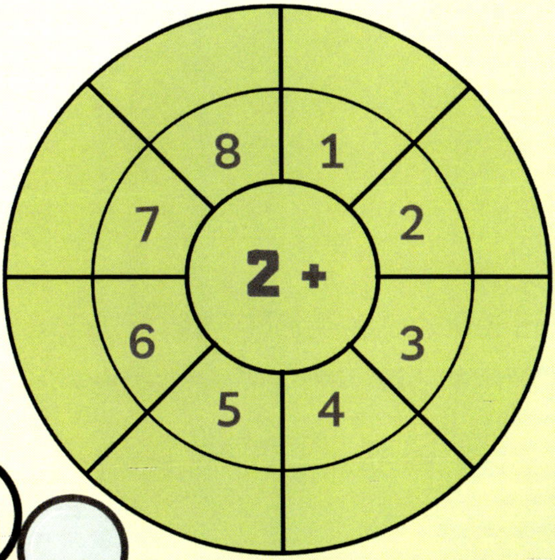

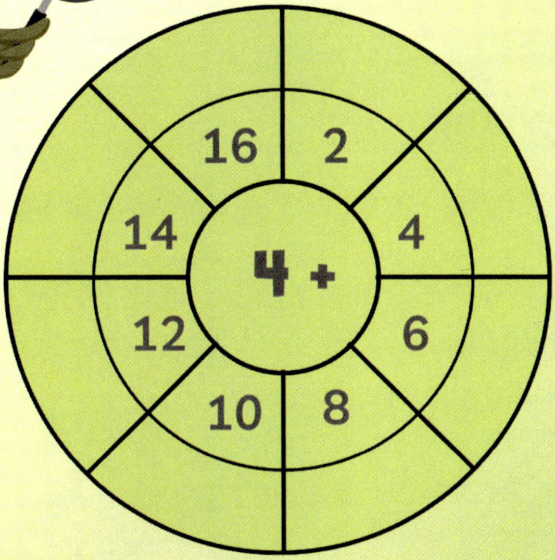

Cardinal and Ordinal Numbers

Cardinal Numbers:

Cardinal numbers are the numbers we use to count things. They tell us how many of something there are. For example, if you have three apples, "three" is a cardinal number because it tells you the quantity of apples you have.

Ordinal Numbers:

Ordinal numbers tell us the position or order of things in a list or series. They help us know which thing comes first, second, third, and so on. For example, if you're in a race and you finish first, second, or third, those numbers are ordinal numbers because they show your place in the race.

Find spellings of the ordinal numbers listed on the right and write the words in spaces provide

S	E	V	E	N	T	H	A	G	E	N	Q	U
S	I	X	T	H	T	H	I	R	D	L	M	B
V	R	P	Q	H	U	F	O	U	R	T	H	L
T	W	E	N	T	Y	F	I	R	S	T	R	T
H	J	Y	K	C	Y	O	H	Q	J	G	B	K
N	I	N	T	H	V	S	E	C	O	N	D	M
U	B	Q	D	T	Q	Q	F	I	R	S	T	Q
M	A	A	T	W	E	N	T	I	E	T	H	P
H	X	T	H	I	R	T	Y	F	I	R	S	T
T	W	E	N	T	Y	S	E	C	O	N	D	T
E	I	G	H	T	H	O	G	X	F	I	O	H
J	D	T	H	I	R	T	I	E	T	H	H	F
L	F	I	F	T	H	D	T	E	N	T	H	C

1st = First

2nd = ...

3rd = ...

4th = ...

5th = ...

6th = ...

7th = ...

8th = ...

9th = ...

10th = ...

20th = ...

21st = ...

22nd = ...

30th = ...

31st = ...

The Magic Box

Use the numbers 4 to 12 to complete the Magic box. The sums of each row, column and diagonal are the same. Write the totals outside the box at the end of each line .

7		11
	8	
5		

Painting by Addition

Paint this picture by figuring out each equation. Use the colour given for colouring each sum.

Ordering Numbers

Ordering numbers is like putting them in the right order, from smallest to biggest or from biggest to smallest. Imagine you have a line of toys, and you want to organize them neatly. When you're ordering numbers, you're doing the same thing but with numbers! You look at the numbers and see which one is the smallest, then you find the next smallest one, and so on until you reach the biggest number. It's like arranging toys from the shortest to the tallest. Ordering numbers helps us understand how things compare to each other and makes math easier to understand!

ASCENDING ORDER

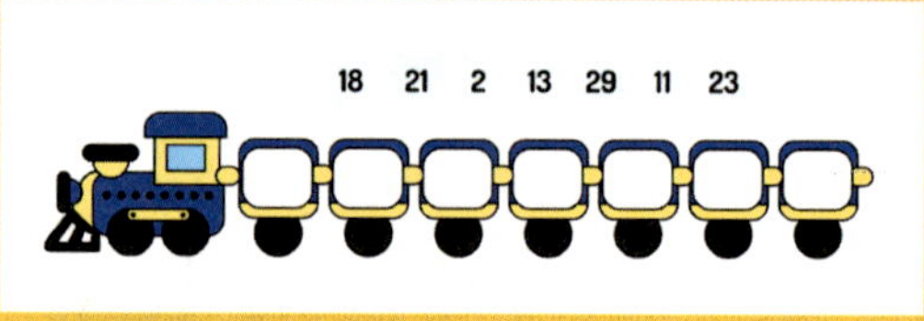

DESCENDING ORDER

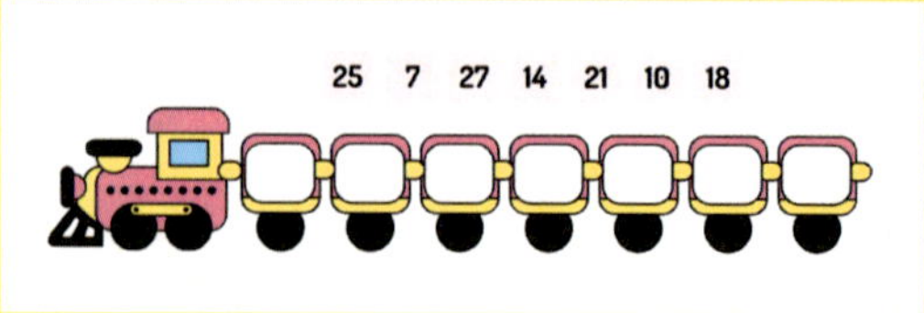

Subtration

Subtraction is like magic math that helps us figure out how many things are left when we take some away. Imagine you have a big pile of yummy cookies. If you eat some of them, subtraction helps you figure out how many cookies are left.

The Subtraction Table

You can also "loop up" answers for simple subtraction using this table

The Subtration Table

-	0	1	2	3	4	5	6	7	8	9	10	11	12
0	0												
1	1	0											
2	2	1	0										
3	3	2	1	0									
4	4	3	2	1	0								
5	5	4	3	2	1	0							
6	6	5	4	3	2	1	0						
7	7	6	5	4	3	2	1	0					
8	8	7	6	5	4	3	2	1	0				
9	9	8	7	6	5	4	3	2	1	0			
10	10	9	8	7	6	5	4	3	2	1	0		
11	11	10	9	8	7	6	5	4	3	2	1	0	
12	12	11	10	9	8	7	6	5	4	3	2	1	0

Practice your Subtraction

Take Away

What's the opposite of 'addtiion?' Subtraction, of course. 'Subtraction' means to take away. If you have 5 oranges and you take away 2 of them, you have 3 oranges left. Easy! Simples" the 'different.' If your little sister is 4 years old and you're 11, then the 'difference' in years between the two of you is 7.

Subtraction Tangles

Complete each of the equation on a separate pices of paper. Then see if you can follow the line to the correct answer

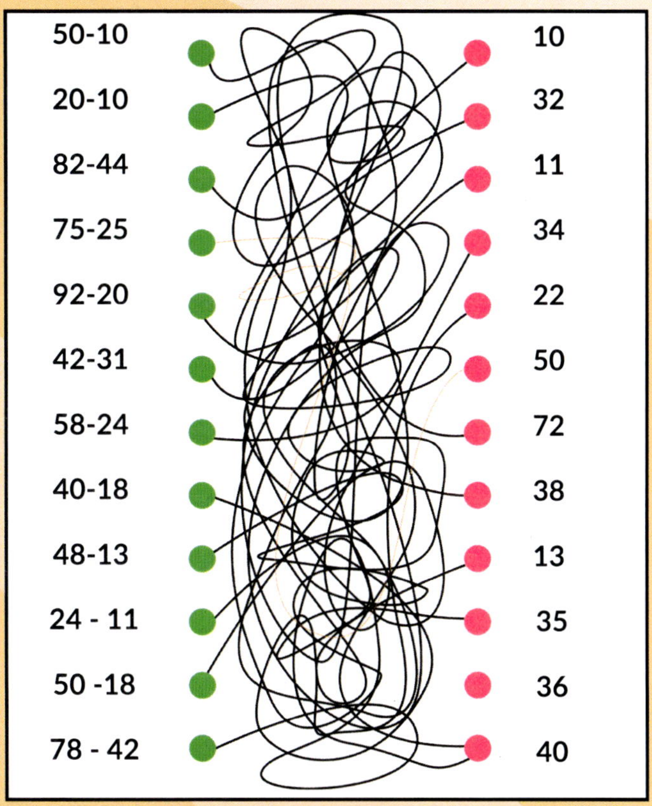

Subtraction Boxes

- The point of each puzzle is to fill in the grid with numbers.
- The only numbers you may write are 1,2,3,4,5.
- No number may appear more than once in any row or column.
- When you see a heavy border that means there's a 'target number'. That number is in the left-hand corner of a box. All the numbers within the heavy border must equal the traget number. You have to use only subtraction.
- Numbers may be repeated in the border are as long asd they do not repeat within a single row or coloum.
- Some boxes have been filled in with numbers

5	-3		2	3
4	2	-1	5	1
1	4		-1	
3	-4		2	
2	3	-4		4

-2		5	-2	
-4		2	4	3
-2	4	3	2	-2
	-4		2	
2	3	1	-2	

Matchstick Madness

Take away some matchstick to make the equation correct.

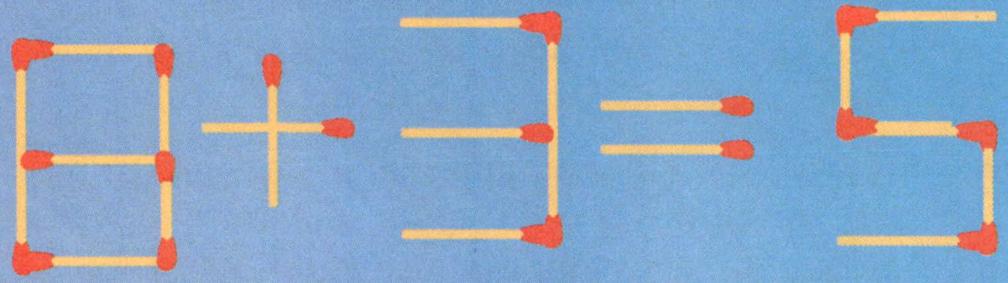

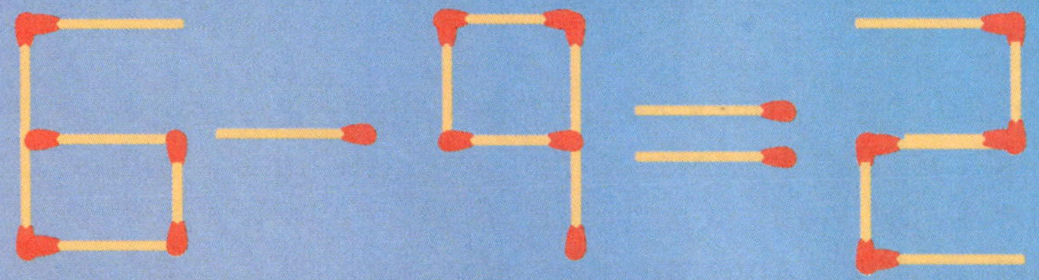

Take away some matchstick to make the equation correct.

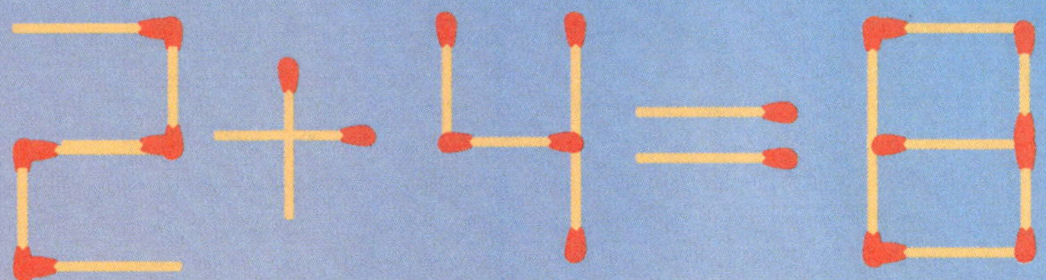

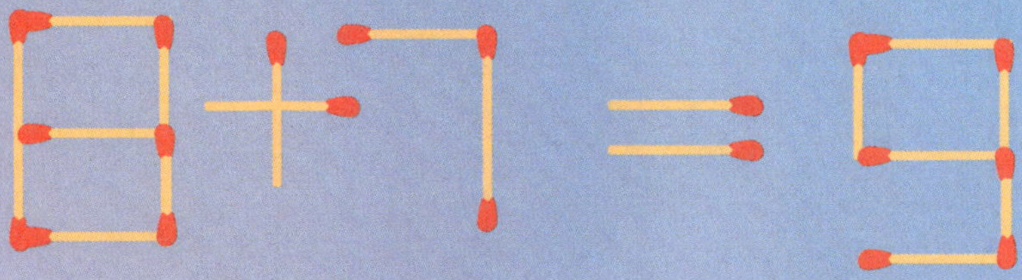

Multiplication

Multiplication is a really handy way of adding numbers together quickly. Imagine you have a bunch of groups of things, like apples. Multiplication helps us figure out how many apples we have in total without counting them one by one.

Let's say you have 3 groups of apples, and each group has 4 apples. Instead of counting each apple one by one (which could take a long time!), you can use multiplication. You multiply the number of groups (3) by the number of apples in each group (4).

In multiplication, we use a special sign called the multiplication sign, which looks like this: ×. So, if you want to multiply 3 groups by 4 apples in each group, you write it like this: 3 × 4. Now, you multiply the numbers together: 3 × 4 = 12. So, you have 12 apples in total! Multiplication helps us quickly find out how many things we have when we have groups of the same amount. It's like a shortcut for adding up lots of things at once!

Some numbers have fallen out of this multiplication table . See if you can them in the correct places.

x	1	2	3	4	5	6	7	8	9	10
1	1	2	3		5	6	7	8	9	10
2	2	4		8	10	12		16		20
3	3	6	9		15	18	21	24	27	30
4	4		12	16	20		28		36	
5	5	10		20	25	30	35	40		50
6	6	12	18	24	30	36	42		54	60
7	7	14	21	28		42	49	56	63	
8	8		24	32	40	48	56	64		80
9	9	18		36	45	54		72	81	90
10		20	30	40		60	70	80	90	100

70 45 32 40 12 50 18 72 4 6 15 24 10 16 60 8 24 48 35 18 14 18

Balancing things Out

When things are equal, they balance ech other out. See if you can figure out this puzzle. The answers are in the back of the book

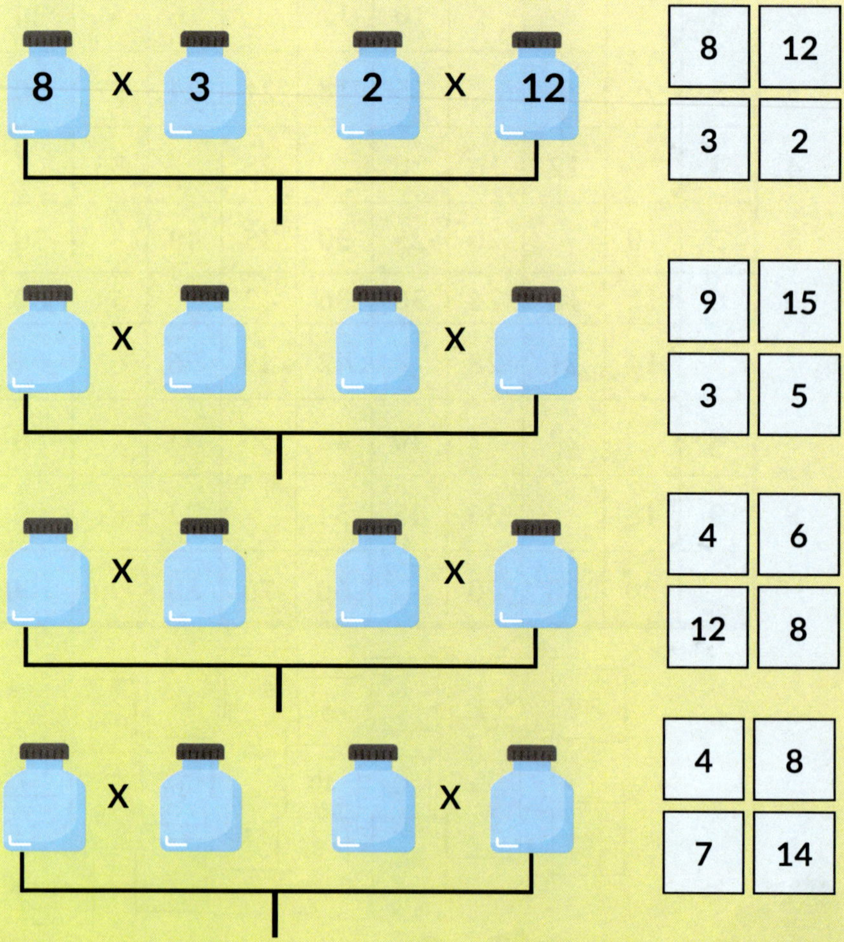

Pattern and Sequences

Pattern are all arount us! Finding and understanding patterns gives us great power. With patterns we learjn to discover new things and better understand the world around us.

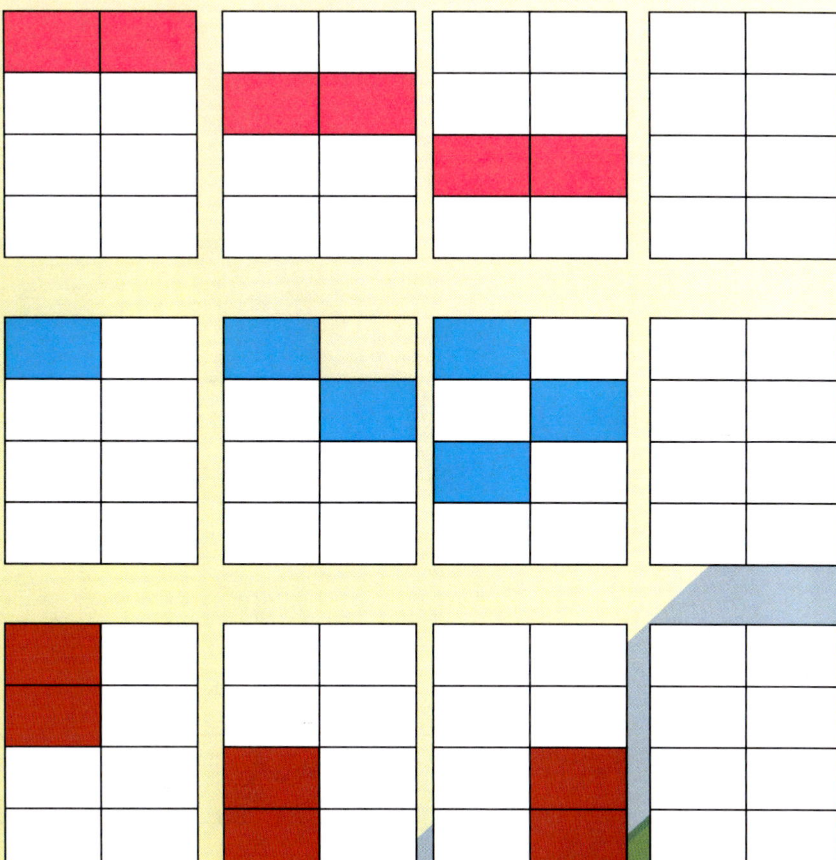

Multiply The Boxes

The point of each puzzle is too fill in the grid with numbers.

- The only numbers you may write 1, 2, 3, 4, 5.
- No numbers may appear more than once in any row or column.
- When you see a heavy border that means there's target number.' That number is in the left-hand corner of a box. All the numbers within the heavy border must equal the target number you have to use only multiplication.
- Numbers may be repeated in the border area as long a they to not repeat within a single row or column.
- some boxes have been filled in with numbers.

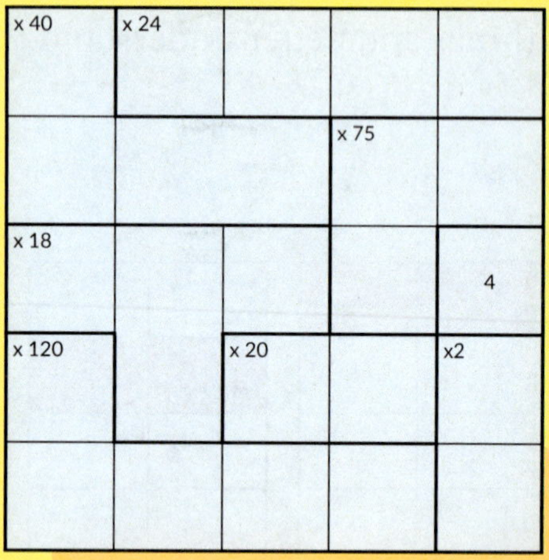

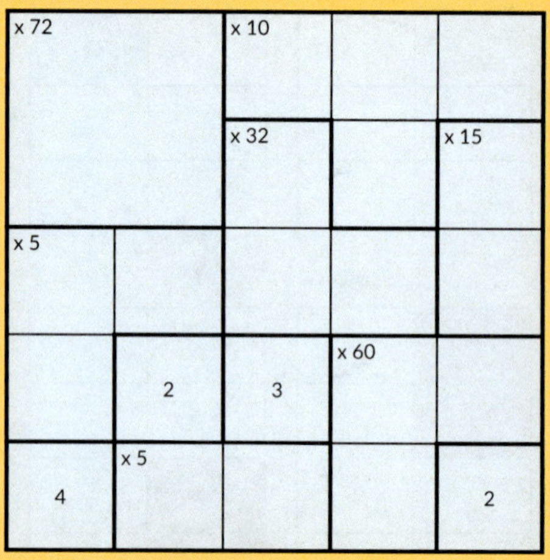

Colourful Fractions

Colour the shapes to represent the fraction.

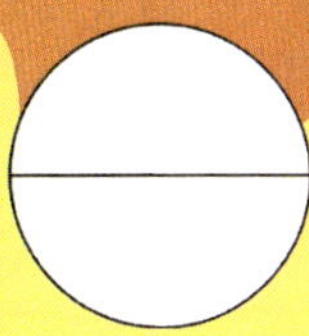

$\frac{1}{2}$

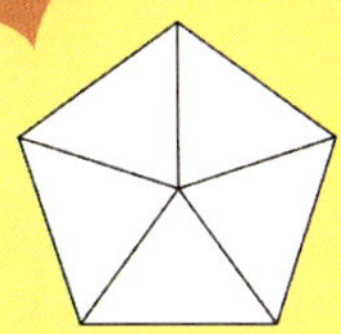

$\frac{2}{5}$

$\frac{1}{5}$

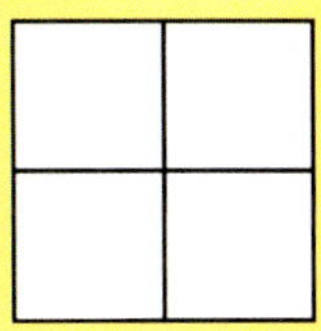

$\frac{3}{4}$

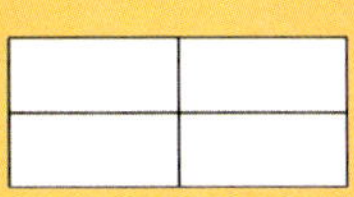

$\frac{1}{2}$

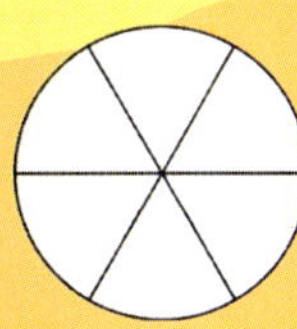

$\frac{5}{6}$

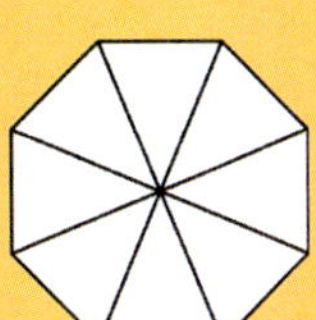

$\frac{3}{8}$

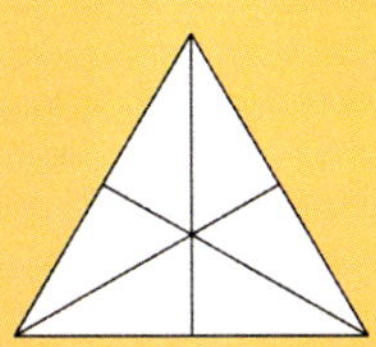

$\frac{1}{6}$

$\frac{1}{4}$

1

Colouring

Colour the triangles according to the instructions below

Shape Up!

Look around you. Go ahead Don't be scared! What to you see? You might see books. You might see a computer screen, or a clock on the wall. Now look a bit closer. What to you really see? That book is in the shape of a square or a rectangle. The computer could i the shape of a rectangle. As for the clock, can you guess what that is? If you said a circle, you'd be right.

Math is more than than numbers. It's also about shapes and points and lines. In other words, it's also about geometry.

Some shapes are flat. They hae length and width, but no thickness. Some shapes are 3-dimensional. That means they hage length, width, and thickness.

Here are some hasic geometric shapes

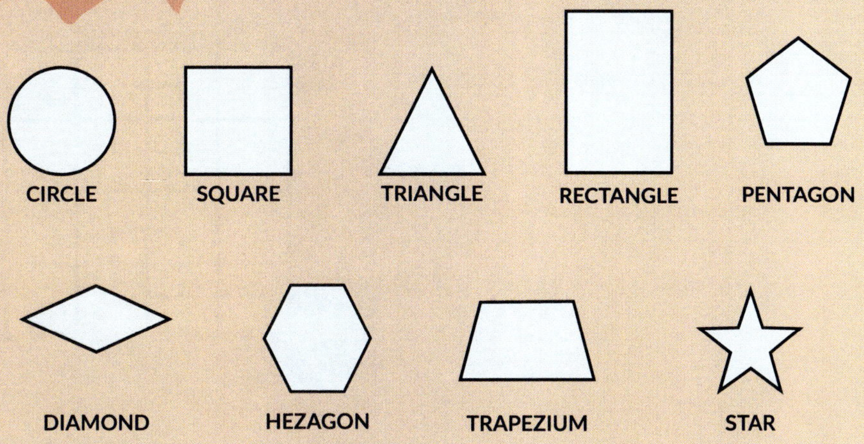

Is Your Mind in Shape?

Put your mind to work and see if you can solve these brain treases.

1 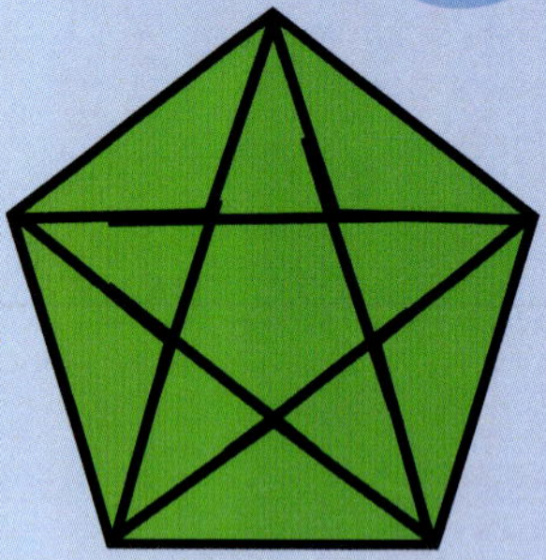

How many triangles can you conut ?

2 Can you move 2 toothpiks to ctreate 7 squares?

3

How many square can you conut ?

4

How many triangles can you conut ?

5

How many square can you find ?

Going the Distance

Distance is a way of measuring how far apart things are from each other. It's like figuring out how much space there is between two points.

Imagine you're going for a walk or a run. The distance you cover is how far you travel from where you start to where you end up. It's like measuring how many steps you take from one place to another.

When you ride in a car or on a bike, you're moving from one place to another, right? The distance you travel is how far you go from your starting point to your destination. We can use tools to help us measure distance more accurately.

We measure distance using different units, like meters, kilometers, feet, or miles. It's like using different kinds of coins to buy things - you can use meters for short distances, and kilometers for longer distances.

Distance isn't just about how far things are on Earth. It's also used to measure how far apart planets are in space! Astronauts travel huge distances when they go to space.

Measuring Word Search

Find these hidden words in the puzzle. All related to units of measurement.

INCH
MILE
FOOT
MILLIMETRE
CENTIMETRE
KILOMETRE
YARD
FURLONG
FATHOM
HAND
ROD
CUBIT
DIGIT
PACE

R	X	H	J	Y	T	L	Q	C	U	G	L	B	I	C	H	H	S
P	E	A	F	U	R	L	O	N	G	M	I	L	E	Q	X	A	A
G	U	N	T	R	I	J	F	B	U	Q	R	C	C	P	G	C	Y
I	I	D	Y	G	P	Q	G	U	V	B	N	J	X	I	K	D	A
K	I	L	O	M	E	T	R	E	Z	E	Q	T	N	W	E	T	R
I	S	M	I	L	L	I	M	E	T	R	E	Z	C	M	U	O	D
O	Y	X	U	R	G	Q	O	K	Z	T	V	R	P	U	N	M	B
K	K	E	I	X	P	N	Y	F	A	T	H	O	M	A	B	S	A
J	C	E	N	T	I	M	E	T	R	E	Y	R	D	E	C	I	Q
A	C	S	C	W	M	C	M	C	T	J	D	I	G	I	T	E	T
I	K	N	H	Z	I	W	J	W	N	V	S	O	R	B	N	E	V
A	F	W	T	S	Z	Z	F	O	O	T	I	J	R	O	D	O	Q

March of Time

At some point in life, you learned how to tell, time, it's an important skill. You learned the difference between minutes, hours, days, weeks months and years. Without a way to tell time, the world would be chaotic.

How do you tell time? If you're like most people, you look at a clock or a watch. But did you know we can also measure time by the circular motions of the moon. Earth

to go around the sun. Everu day, Earth spine on its axis. It takes 24 hours, or 1 day, for that to happen. Each hour of the day is 60 minutes. There are 60 seconds in each minutes

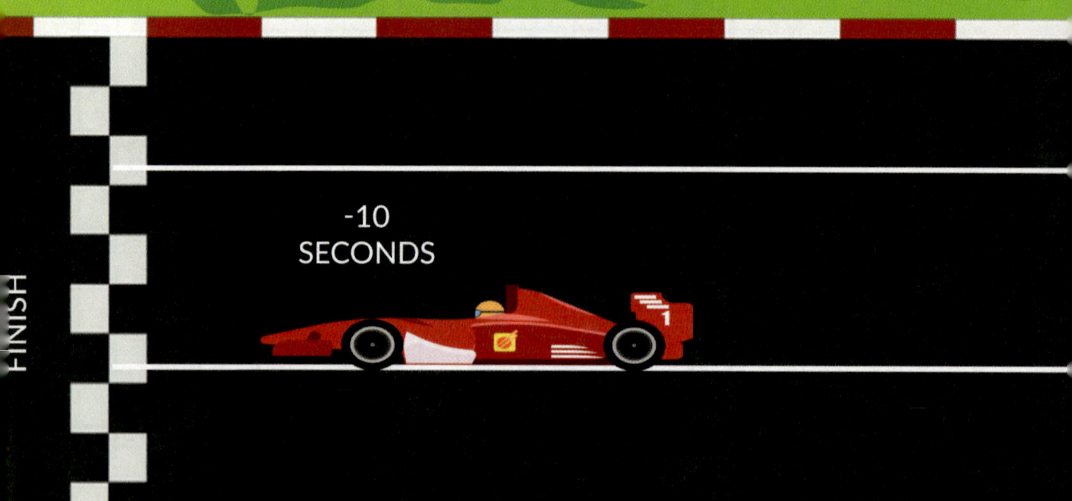

On Time!

Knowingn how to tell time keeps you from being late for school or late for supper. it also helps people know who wins a car race. Can you help race official figure out the time the yellow and bule cars crosssed the finish line? The time for the blue car is noted. You need to figure out how much faster or slower the other cars were write down each time next to each car.

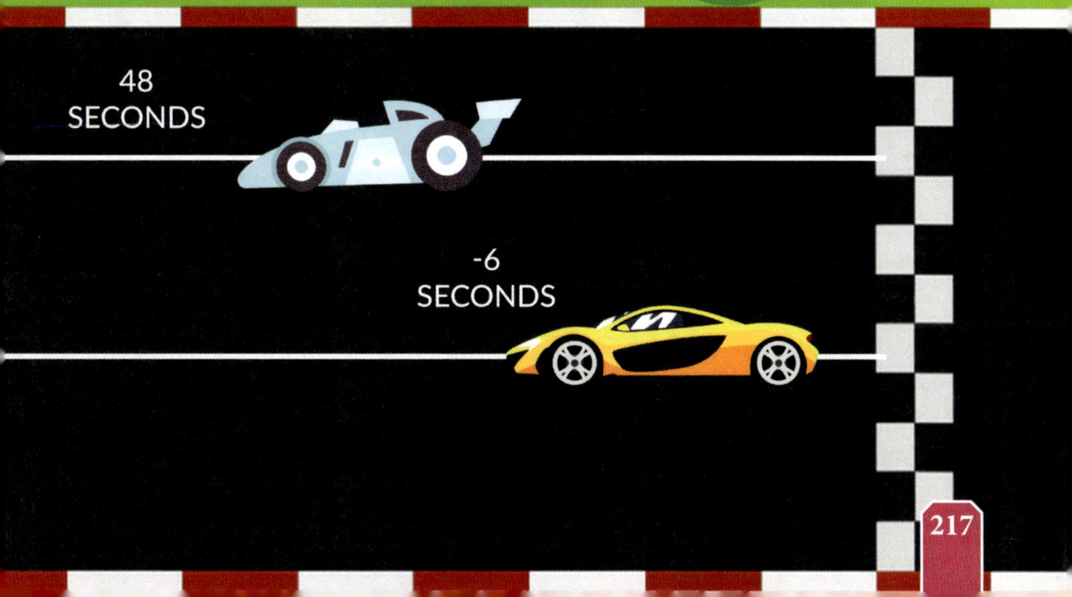

Grate Graphs

A graph us drawing or a diagram that shows information, or data. There are four different types of graphs : bar, pictoraph, line and circle.

Ice-Cream Sales

Study the bar graph and then answer the questions that follow.

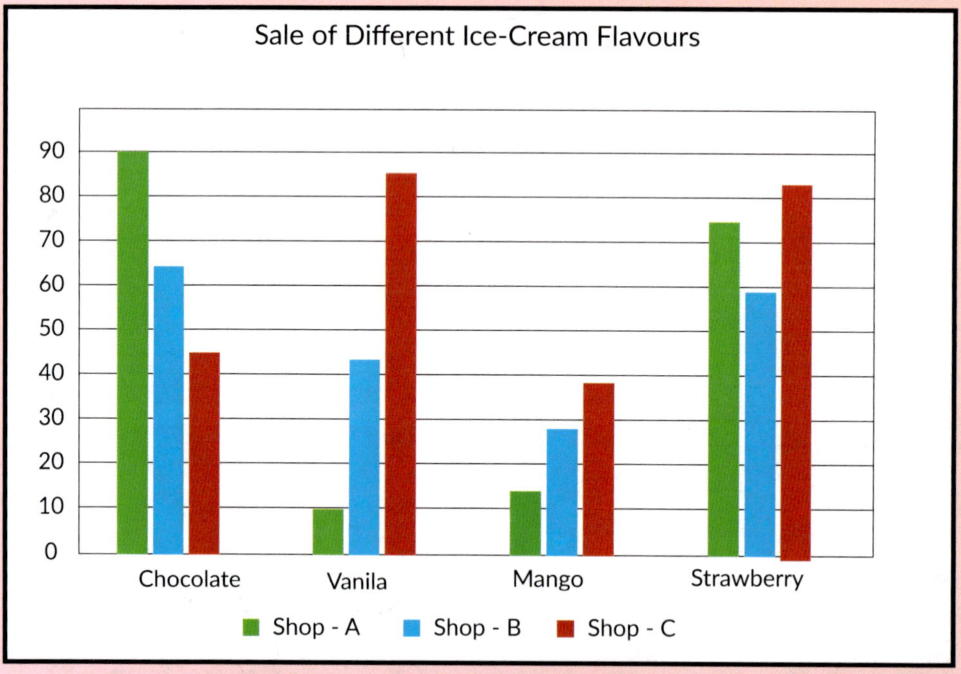

1. Which shop sold the most chocolate ice creame?
2. How many more strawberry ice creams did shop C sell than Shop B?
3. Which shop sold the most ice creams?
4. From this information, which ice-cream flavour is the least popular?

Symmetry

Many things in the world are symmetrical. That means if you cut that thing in half, is the same. The easiest way to think of symmetry is to look at your reflection n the mirror

The Same on Each Side

Complete the picture

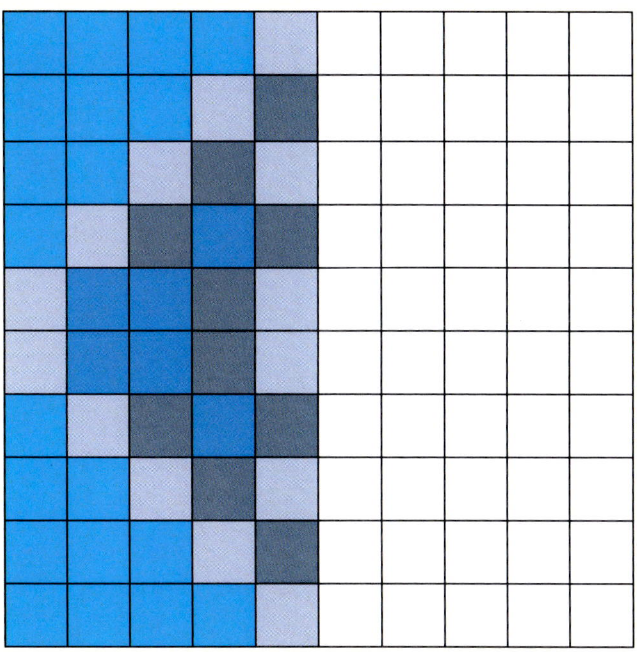

Measurement

Measurement is a skill to compare objects in terms of their shapes and sizes. You can compare two objects based on their 'Height', Size and 'Weight. Height helps you tell whether the objects are 'Tall or Short'. Size tells you whether the objects are 'Thick or Thin and weight tell you whether the objects are 'Heavy or Light?

Tools for Measurement

An object can be measured using tools like ruler, scales and weighing scales.

(a)

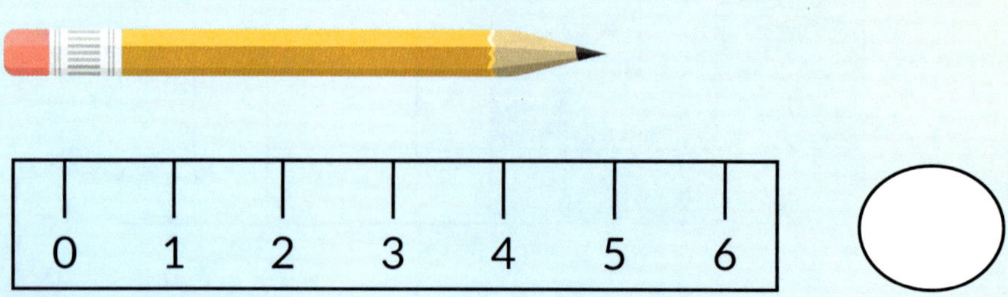

(b)

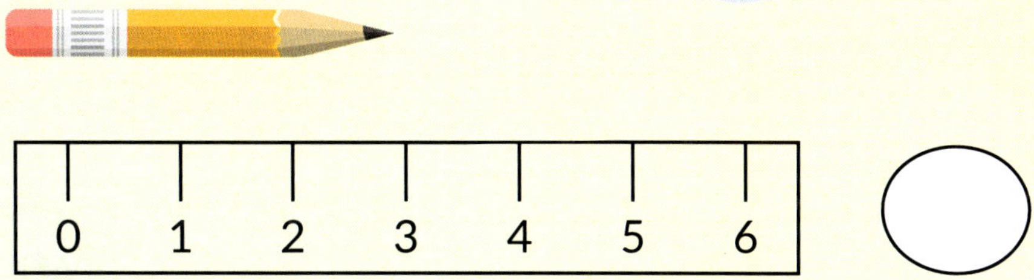

(c)

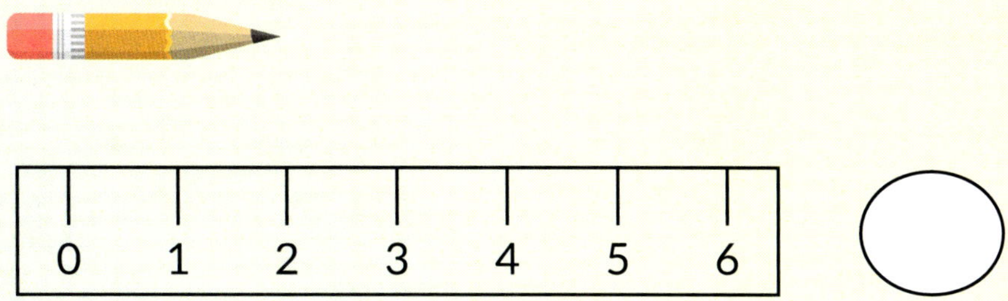

(d)

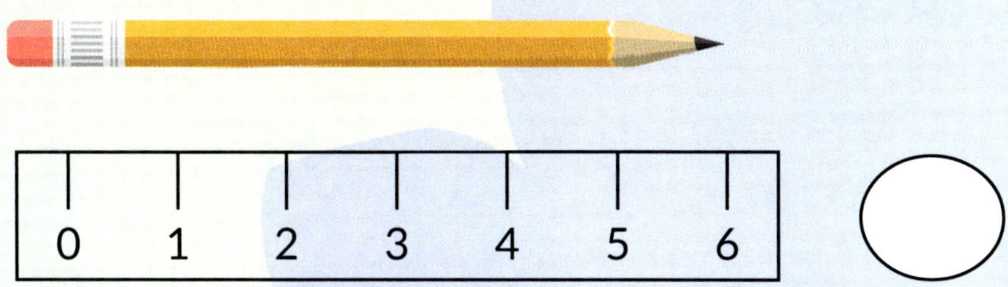

Time

Time is the ongoing sequence of events taking place. The past, present and future. We measure time using seconds, minutes, hours, days, weeks, months and years. Clocks

Showing the Time

There are two main ways to show the time:

"24 Hour Clock" or AM/PM.

......8 : 00......   ...... : .... : ......

...... : .... : .... : ......

The AM/PM

AM/PM (or "12 Hour Clock"): the day is split into:

- the 12 Hours running from Midnight to Noon (the AM hours), and
- the other 12 Hourse running from Noon to midnight (the PM hours

1. The time is 9:30 in the morning is it AM or PM?

2. You went out for shopping along with your mom in the evening is it AM or PM

ANSWERS

ANSWERS

SCIENCE

PAGE -17

A	L	E	X	A	N	D	E	R	F	L	E	M	I	N	G	M
L	L	O	U	I	S	P	A	S	T	E	U	R	K	I	L	A
N	I	R	F	Q	Z	C	W	X	L	L	R	F	Z	B	A	R
I	S	G	Y	S	B	G	Y	H	G	K	Z	R	S	T	L	I
K	A	T	H	O	M	A	S	E	D	I	S	O	N	O	F	E
O	A	I	D	P	J	X	R	K	O	A	K	J	E	E	R	C
L	C	O	W	O	A	H	N	P	O	L	G	J	A	D	E	U
A	N	T	V	R	M	N	R	A	E	A	B	J	C	W	D	R
T	E	A	L	B	E	R	T	E	I	N	S	T	E	I	N	I
E	W	Y	H	M	S	E	X	O	O	T	S	H	B	N	O	E
S	T	B	E	E	W	Y	H	O	R	U	E	O	N	H	B	H
L	O	H	P	F	A	P	A	S	L	R	M	M	A	U	E	N
A	N	O	R	D	T	O	Z	S	D	I	Q	S	H	B	L	M
J	M	L	Q	E	S	U	S	B	X	N	A	O	I	B	L	S
N	S	B	H	Y	O	S	I	L	Q	G	S	N	R	L	P	X
M	D	M	H	E	N	O	B	E	I	M	M	V	N	E	P	J
E	R	N	E	S	T	R	U	T	H	E	R	F	O	R	D	G
M	B	U	A	U	V	T	C	L	B	W	F	E	H	V	W	P
Q	M	S	T	E	P	H	E	N	H	A	W	K	I	N	G	P
N	Y	V	O	F	N	F	C	W	T	W	L	R	N	F	T	R
X	H	V	S	X	R	Y	F	Y	A	S	K	X	R	T	H	C
C	H	A	R	L	E	S	D	A	R	W	I	N	J	U	Y	Q

PAGE -22

(a)Fur

(b) Feather

(c)Scale

(d) Scale

(e) Scale

(f) Scale

(g)Fur

(h) Scale

PAGE -23

Examples of Vertebrates are:
Frog, Fish, Sheep, Panda, Flamingo, Crocodile

PAGE -31

(1) Crust
(2) Mantel Outer
(3) Outer Core
(4) Inner Core

PAGE -37

1. The building shook.
2. Earth moved under my feet.
3. The Walls fell down.
4. Mom's china cracked.

PAGE -39

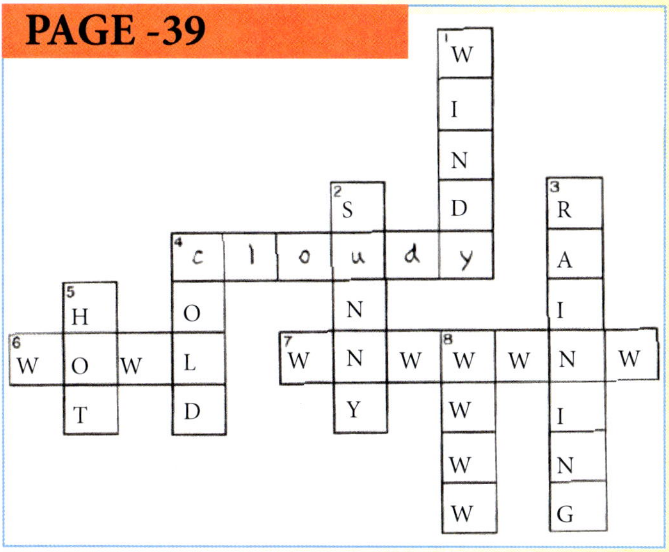

PAGE -41

h	l	d	o	p	y	b	z	e	n	j	g	e	I	d
z	z	a	x	I	w	R	n	R	a	I	n	y	I	o
w	n	x	n	I	b	a	R	o	m	e	t	e	R	o
a	t	I	u	d	c	p	l	R	d	b	w	q	f	l
h	e	x	d	I	f	u	l	l	l	e	n	n	u	f
e	a	n	R	m	k	a	x	c	l	t	I	R	k	e
o	I	R	x	e	c	c	l	y	l	a	d	s	v	s
w	u	t	b	a	k	m	a	l	n	t	e	t	v	t
h	z	f	a	s	n	z	s	a	g	u	j	z	l	t
I	t	f	d	u	g	I	t	y	t	b	b	R	k	c
f	k	s	a	R	m	u	I	u	m	w	j	a	f	u
m	q	x	k	e	R	R	v	c	y	b	w	j	m	v
n	n	x	d	e	a	a	O	R	I	q	a	d	o	z
x	c	h	g	a	c	k	y	t	a	f	d	t	w	e
y	q	R	n	q	I	l	g	b	s	v	z	j	l	m

PAGE -45

PAGE -47

PAGE -57

(a) Solid
(b) Liquid
(c) Gas

(a) Solid to liquid
(b) Liquid to gas
(c) Gas to liquid

PAGE -59

(a) PE
(b) KE
(c) PE
(d) Both
(e) PE
(f) Both

ANSWERS
TECHNOLOGY

PAGE -62

PAGE -63

PAGE -65

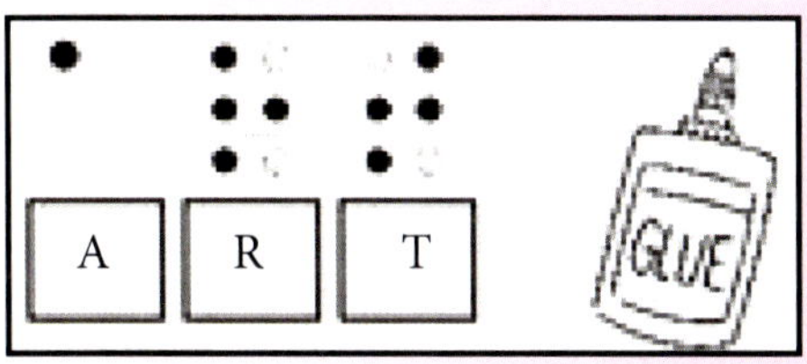

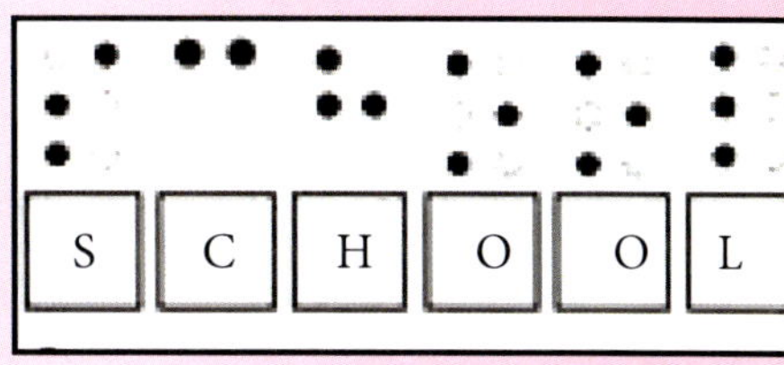

PAGE -71

Q.1 **Remote controls are ____ objects.**

1. Wireless. 2. Wired.
3. Both (1) and (2). 4. None of the above.

Q.2 **____ is sent as a signal to convey our actions to another device.**

1. Waves. 2. Lines.
3. Dots. 4. Sound.

Q.3. ___ are transmitted by the remote of remote-controlled toy.

1. Radio waves. 2. Infrared waves.
3. X-ray waves. 4. None of the above.

PAGE -77

A		S	I	N	C	E	R	E		H	E	A	R	T		W	I	T	H
3		4	9	11	1	5	15	5		14	5	3	15	6		12	9	6	14

R	E	A	L		I	N	T	E	N	T		H	A	V	I	N	G
15	5	3	16		9	11	6	5	11	6		14	3	10	9	11	7

F	A	I	T	H		I	N		C	H	R	I	S	T
2	3	9	6	14		9	11		1	14	15	9	4	6

PAGE -79

DNA THEMED WORD SEARCH

M	A	J	F	W	H	B	P	H	E	R	S	H	E	Y	A	Y	C
C	U	D	Q	F	T	L	A	Y	D	N	A	P	G	J	Y	M	H
P	Y	T	E	I	W	N	G	S	R	A	L	L	E	L	E	C	R
H	H	T	A	N	G	P	T	E	E	I	G	G	A	A	C	H	O
I	G	E	O	T	O	U	R	M	N	P	M	E	J	S	N	A	M
P	E	C	N	S	I	S	A	O	E	O	A	I	N	U	J	S	O
U	N	R	U	O	I	O	I	N	T	N	T	I	D	O	H	E	S
R	E	I	M	O	T	N	N	N	I	E	D	Y	R	I	M	J	O
I	O	C	E	T	N	Y	E	J	E	N	I	E	P	S	N	E	M
N	L	K	I	H	J	O	P	Z	N	G	E	N	L	E	F	E	E
E	R	J	Z	N	U	C	L	E	O	T	I	D	E	A	Y	T	B
U	T	R	R	E	P	L	I	C	A	T	I	O	N	B	W	M	U

ANSWERS
ENGINEERING

PAGE -97

Examples of inclined plane are: a, c, e

PAGE -99

A. yes
B. yes
C. yes
D. no
E. yes
F. no
G. yes

PAGE -101

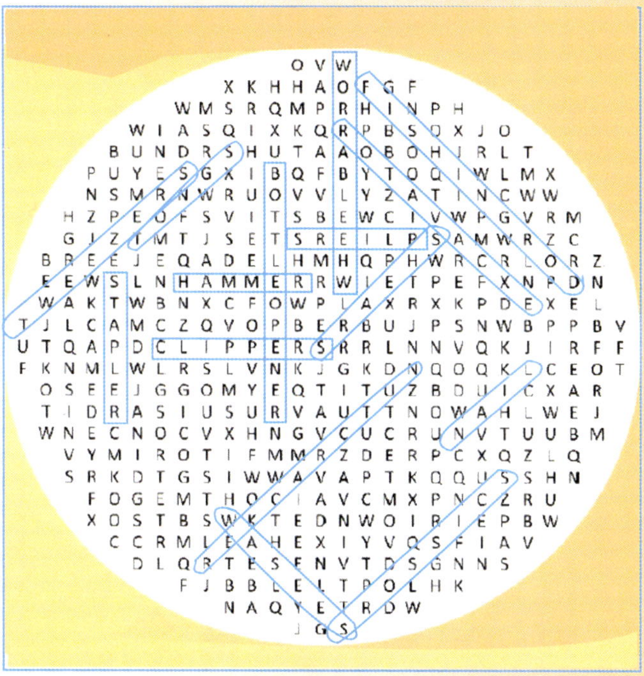

PAGE -105

B			C	A	R	J	A	C	K			D
												R
		L										I
		I	T									L
		G										L
		H										B
B	O	T	T	L	E	T	O	P				I
		B										T
F	A	U	C	E	T							
		L										
		B					J	A	R	L	I	D

PAGE -107

Examples of pulley are:
a, c, d, f, g

PAGE -117

Famous Skyscrapers

V X U S J I N M A O T O W E R N C I O F M S Z O
T H B H A Y E K G N I K T G A E L R O C A K M Q
M F M M Q K C W Z V J G R L O T T E D N E O R A
Z A T I R E T N E C N A H U W N V X O Z F N A V
O N T U U N F Z D A E D Q I M T X R U U U E S O
Q I D U G B F R U H V X U M A L T D O G S W Y I
L R Z S K Q I G W R D I D I P E U H X M J O E M
O A M K E G N K G N G E P J P A Z G I S S R R I
D M G N X W A V V J A E Y I T G O Z Z W T L G C
W G E N G C N O N Z I G I O N R R M X F J D Y C
Q U E O H C C T Q B P P N A L K A C M X T T I B
S T G B U Z E Q U Q R X U I M J M Z U X O R S U
E M H L J F D B G P C G Z Y P D T U U R I A U R
U F N B X U O R W N M O C F Z C H D N Z I D G J
W V A B R A J A L B A I T C L O C K T O W E R K
N P R E W O T S I L L I W Z Z Y Y Y X K C C C H
S F T X H D I A H G N A H S B T T I D J E E S A
Y K N F E O A A D S Q D N B A K G O D B O N U L
A A D U I R E W O T G N E F I Z U T E S Q T K I
Q W G N I D L I U B E T A T S E R I P M E E N F
P A R K A V E N U E N T O N V F P L M G H R G A
T R U M P T O W E R W G W S Y K P F A I O G Z F
X D J C Z N N C C Y X V B F T S U F L A P L L Z
N Q D D C Y O U K K Z P L T W O Y D W V J Y H Q

PAGE -121

(a) three years

(b) southeast

PAGE -123

(a) Clipper
(b) Submarine
(c) Gallev
(d) Rope
(e) Deck

PAGE -129

PAGE -133

(a) My T-Shirt
(b) Enjoying a hot chocolate
(c) Cold

PAGE -141

ANSWERS

MATHS

PAGE -179

V	VI	II	I	IV	III
IV	III	I	II	V	VI
VI	IV	III	V	I	2
II	I	V	III	VI	IV
III	V	VI	IV	II	I
I	II	IV	VI	III	V

PAGE -180

2	5	9	3	1	4	7	6	8
8	7	1	6	2	9	4	5	3
6	4	3	5	8	7	1	9	2
9	6	7	8	3	5	2	1	4
4	1		9	7		5	3	6
	2	5	4	6	1	9	8	7
7	9	6	2	5	3	8	4	1
1	8	4	7	5	6	3	2	5
5	3	2	1	4	8	6	7	4

PAGE -181

(a)  12, Even

(b)  13, Odd

(c)  10, Even

PAGE -183

 > 

 = 

 > 

 = 

 > 

PAGE -184

+11 5	3	+10 1	4	+6 2
3	+6 1	2	5	4
+9 4	5	3	**2**	**1**
+5 1	2	4	+9 3	5
2	+13 4	5	1	**3**

+9 2	4	+9 5	3	+5 1
3	+7 5	2	1	4
+10 5	1	4	**2**	**3**
1	+5 2	3	4	5
+8 4	3	1	+7 5	**2**

PAGE -185

+8 5	2	+7 3	4	+6 1
1	+11 3	4	5	2
2	4	+6 5	1	3
+8 3	5	+7 1	2	4
+5 4	1	2	+8 3	5

PAGE -186

		10 + 2 12	6 + 4 10	11 + 1 12	10 + 5 15
12 + 2 14	4 + 3 7	11 + 7 18	1 + 2 3	4 + 4 8	7 + 2 9
13 + 1 14	4 + 8 12	2 + 10 12	9 + 1 10	7 + 1 8	14 + 3 17
6 + 2 8	3 + 7 10	7 + 4 11	9 + 4 13	3 + 3 6	13 + 3 16
8 + 2 10	4 + 11 15	3 + 5 8	1 + 7 8	8 + 2 10	15 + 1 16
5 + 7 6	5 + 5 10	9 + 3 12	9 + 9 18		

PAGE -187

10 + 1 11	14 + 3 17	3 + 8 11	10 + 8 18	14 + 5 19	
1 + 6 7	12 + 2 14			9 + 3 12	16 + 1 17
5 + 2 7	6 + 11 17	12 + 4 16	3 + 3 6	6 + 1 7	15 + 2 17
11 + 1 12	2 + 15 17	2 + 9 11	3 + 16 19	4 + 3 7	7 + 7 14
12 + 1 13	1 + 8 9	6 + 5 11	1 + 5 6	3 + 14 17	8 + 7 15
14 + 2 16	5 + 9 14	6 + 1 7	9 + 8 17	4 + 7 11	10 + 8 17

PAGE -189

2 sets of 4 = 8

2 sets of 3 = 4

3 sets of 4 = 16

PAGE -192

1	2	3	4	5
6	7	8	9	10
	11	12	13	14
		15	16	17
		18	19	20

PAGE -190

15 + 35	57
17 + 40	68
22 + 33	95
36 + 28	88
10 + 12	56
43 + 52	64
34 + 54	22
18 + 38	55
32 + 35	39
24 + 15	67
18 + 50	30

PAGE -193

PAGE -195

S	E	V	E	N	T	H	A	G	E	N	Q	U
S	I	X	T	H	T	H	I	R	D	L	M	B
V	R	P	Q	H	U	F	O	U	R	T	H	L
T	W	E	N	T	Y	F	I	R	S	T	R	T
H	J	Y	K	C	Y	O	H	Q	J	G	B	K
N	I	N	T	H	V	S	E	C	O	N	D	M
U	B	Q	D	T	Q	Q	F	I	R	S	T	Q
M	A	A	T	W	E	N	T	I	E	T	H	P
H	X	T	H	I	R	T	Y	F	I	R	S	T
T	W	E	N	T	Y	S	E	C	O	N	D	T
E	I	G	H	T	H	O	G	X	F	I	O	H
J	D	T	H	I	R	T	I	E	T	H	H	F
L	F	I	F	T	H	D	T	E	N	T	H	C

PAGE -196

7	6	11
12	8	4
5	10	9

PAGE -198

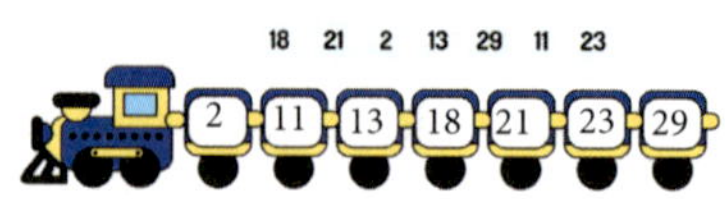

PAGE -200

PAGE -201

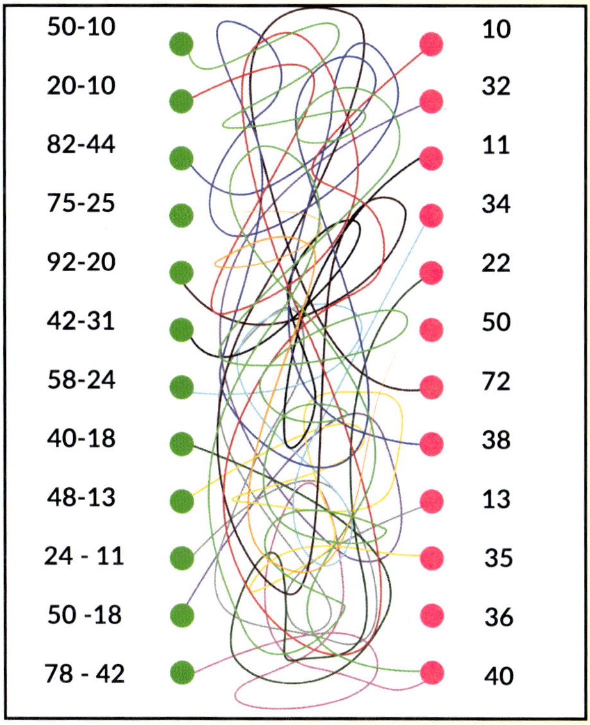

PAGE -202

5	[-3] 1	4	2	3
4	2	[-1] 3	5	1
1	4	2	[-2] 3	5
3	[-4] 5	1	[-2] 4	2
2	3	[-4] 5	1	4

[-2] 4	2	5	[-2] 3	1
[-4] 5	1	2	4	3
[-2] 1	4	3	2	[-2] 5
3	5	[-3]	2	2
2	3	1	[-1] 5	4

PAGE -203

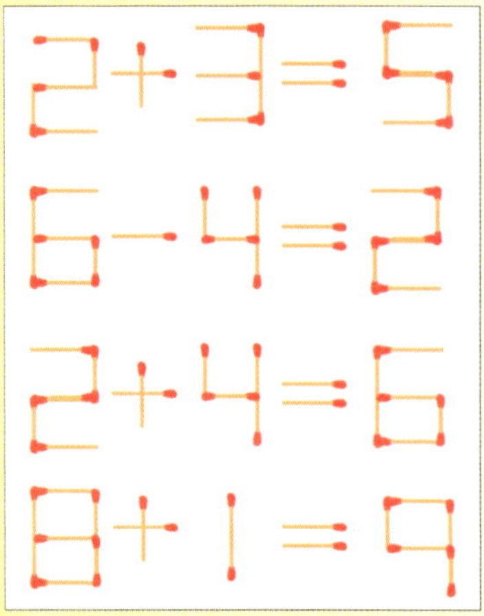

PAGE -205

x	1	2	3	4	5	6	7	8	9	10
1	1	2	3	4	5	6	7	8	9	10
2	2	4	6	8	10	12	14	16	18	20
3	3	6	9	12	15	18	21	24	27	30
4	4	8	12	16	20	24	28	32	36	40
5	5	10	15	20	25	30	35	40	45	50
6	6	12	18	24	30	36	42	48	54	60
7	7	14	21	28	35	42	49	56	63	70
8	8	16	24	32	40	48	56	64	72	80
9	9	18	27	36	45	54	63	72	81	90
10	10	20	30	40	50	60	70	80	90	100

PAGE -206

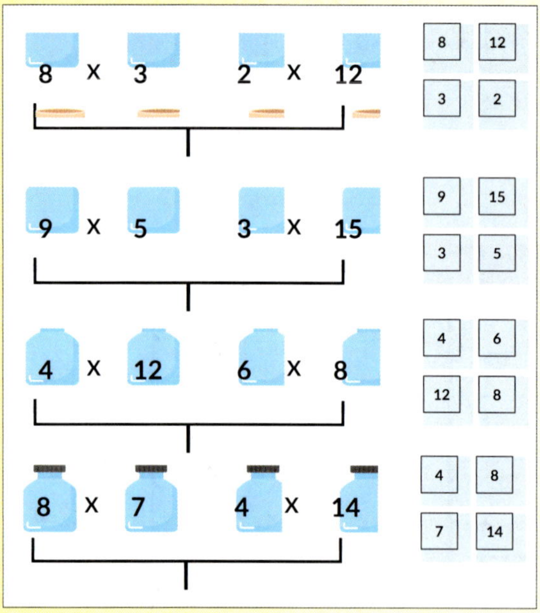

PAGE -207

PAGE -208

x 40 5	x 24 6	2	1	3
4	2	1	x 75 3	5
x 18 2	1	3	5	4
x 120 1	3	x 20 5	4	x2 2
3	5	4	2	1

x 72 3	4	x 10 5	2	1
2	3	x 32 4	1	x 15 5
x 5 5	1	2	4	3
1	2	3	x 60 5	4
4	x 5 5	1	3	2

PAGE -212-213

1. 35 traingles
2 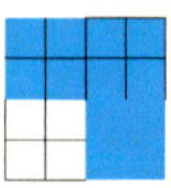
3. 40 Square
4 17 trianges
5. 40 squares

PAGE -215

R	X	H	J	Y	T	L	Q	C	U	G	L	B	I	C	H	H	S
P	E	A	F	U	R	L	O	N	G	M	I	L	E	Q	X	A	A
G	U	N	T	R	I	J	F	B	U	Q	R	C	C	P	G	C	Y
I	I	D	Y	G	P	Q	G	U	V	B	N	J	X	I	K	D	A
K	I	L	O	M	E	T	R	E	Z	E	Q	T	N	W	E	T	R
I	S	M	I	L	L	I	M	E	T	R	E	Z	C	M	U	O	D
O	Y	X	U	R	G	Q	O	K	Z	T	V	R	P	U	N	M	B
K	K	E	I	X	P	N	Y	F	A	T	H	O	M	A	B	S	A
J	C	E	N	T	I	M	E	T	R	E	Y	R	D	E	C	I	Q
A	C	S	C	W	M	C	M	C	T	J	D	I	G	I	T	E	T
I	K	N	H	Z	I	W	J	W	N	V	S	O	R	B	N	E	V
A	F	W	T	S	Z	Z	F	O	O	T	I	J	R	O	D	O	Q

PAGE -216 -217

Red Car - 38 seconds

Yellow Car- 42seconds

PAGE -218

1. Shop = A
2. About 27 More
3. Shop c
4. Mango

PAGE -219

PAGE -220-221

(a) 4 inches
(b) 3 inches
(c) 2 inches
(d) 6 inches

PAGE -222

8 : 00   11 : 00   4 : 00

2 : 00   10 : 00   5 : 00

PAGE -223

1. 9:30 in the morning AM
2. Shoping with mom in the evening PM